BECOME IMMUNE
TO
MANIPULATION

BECOME IMMUNE TO MANIPULATION

HOW THEY ARE MANIPULATING YOU
(AND HOW TO RESIST IT)

NOAH REVOY

Unbreakable Mind Consulting LLC
Redmond, WA

This book is for informational purposes only. It is not intended to serve as a substitute for professional advice. The author and publisher specifically disclaim any and all liability arising directly or indirectly from the use of any information contained in this book. A qualified professional should be consulted regarding your specific situation. Any product mentioned in this book does not imply endorsement of or affiliation with that product by the author or publisher. The conversations in the book are based on the author's recollections, though they are not intended to represent verbatim transcripts. Rather, the author has retold them in a way that communicates the spirit of what was said.

Unbreakable Mind Consulting LLC
21815 NE 81st Street
Redmond, WA 98053
www.unbreakablemindconsulting.com
Send feedback to coach@noahrevoy.com

Publisher's Cataloging-In-Publication Data

    Names: Revoy, Noah, author.
    Title: Become immune to manipulation : how they are manipulating you (and how to resist it) / Noah Revoy.
    Description: Redmond, WA : Unbreakable Mind Consulting LLC, [2022]
    Identifiers: ISBN 9798985953404 (hardcover) | ISBN 9798985953411 (softcover) | ISBN 9798985953428 (ebook)
    Subjects: LCSH: Manipulative behavior. | Persuasion (Psychology) | Interpersonal relations.
    Classification: LCC BF632.5 .R48 2022 (print) | LCC BF632.5 (ebook) | DDC 158.2--dc23

This book is dedicated to my great-grandmother who told me to always, "Follow truth, no matter where it takes you," to my wife Raquel, who has never attempted to manipulate me, and to my son Levi, who at the tender age of five was able to lovingly point out a few remaining places where I was self-manipulating.

Contents

TELL ME WHAT YOU THINK

Let other readers know what you thought of *Become Immune to Manipulation*. Please write an honest review for this book on your favorite online bookshop.

★★★★★

WHAT'S NEXT?

UnbreakableMind

**RESIST MANIPULATION,
PERSUADE WITH INTEGRITY,
AND MAKE PEOPLE DEAL
WITH YOU HONESTLY**

WITH NOAH REVOY

This book reveals the manipulation around you. This new course teaches you what to do about it.

Unbreakable Mind is a video course that trains you to respond to manipulation with persuasion and does so with word-for-word scripts and numerous real-world examples.

In short, what this book tells you, the course shows.

Give yourself an unbreakable mind.

Resist manipulation.

Persuade with integrity.

And make people deal with you honestly.

Readers get 40 percent off– Use discount code IMMUNE.

FOREWORD: THE GLITCH IN MY MATRIX

Most forewords are written by a name you recognize—a celebrity, public figure, or published author. I am none of those. My name is Francis, and I'm a normal, middle-class American like most of you reading this book.

That might surprise you. Most forewords are written by a famous individual with the implicit intent of increasing personal brand awareness. Adding their name to a lesser-known author's book can do just that. Sometimes they write a gushing, praise-laden foreword to repay a private favor.

This foreword is neither of those. This is my customer review, a client testimonial. I hired the author of this book to make me strong against manipulation, and he delivered. When he told me he wanted to write a book to help other people protect themselves the way he'd taught me and asked if I'd write a foreword telling the truth about his methods, I was honored.

I want more people to get the benefit from Noah's book that I have gotten from working with him. His personal coaching has been worth every dime, and getting the benefit of his mind for the price of a book is the deal of a lifetime. To explain why, let me tell you how Noah helped me.

I met Noah a few years ago in an online group dissecting the manipulation framework GSRRM, an acronym for the tactics gossiping, shaming, rallying, ridicule, moralizing, psychologizing, undermining, reputation destruction, and saving face or consent. You'll soon learn more about these. At the time, I was going through a major life transition. A total upheaval of my previous perception of reality. Tons of coworkers at my corporate job suddenly got laid off, and the shock was a glitch in my matrix. I had been taught to believe you could get a job at an established corporation, and the company would take care of you. The company's messaging was exactly that. "Remain loyal to us, everybody gets their share. We're a tribe. *A family.* We're all in this together." Then the layoffs happened.

By benefit of my position, I managed to avoid the axe. But so many people in the tribe whom I trusted and respected were laid off. Thousands and thousands of people were gone at a time of prosperity, when the company was making money hand over fist. People cried.

Some told me they weren't sure how they'd support their families. This was supposed to be a family, but suddenly, they were tossed out in the cold just to cut costs.

That shock was a wake-up call. Tribes don't cast out their own members when everything is going well. That experience made me question the perception of reality I was told not just by a manipulative corporate employer but also from society at large. Who else had been lying to me in order to exploit me? I suddenly questioned everything I had been taught. That's a hard place to be because you go from a comfortable world of blissful ignorance to suddenly realizing how vulnerable you really are.

During my initial search, I came across Nassim Nicholas Taleb. In his books, he discusses Mediocristan and Extremistan—two competing realities. The first is the middle-class operating system; it's what I had installed in me. You play it safe, take little risks, and come out mediocre. But you're dependent on other people (like my corporate employer). The second, Extremistan, selects for giant wins. You can lose ninety-nine times, but one win makes it all worth it.

That definition helped, but I had no idea what to do about it. I wanted to thrive in Extremistan but had no clue how to get there. Meanwhile, I had to maintain my life in Mediocristan and pretend I was fine. I found myself experiencing cognitive dissonance. I further questioned my map of reality. Reality is out there and infinitely complex, and my map had what I'd always thought was an accurate view. But the layoff, Taleb's books, and examples around me made me realize I was using the wrong map.

A former coworker had left the corporation three years prior to found another company—to create a consumer electronics company. Three years later, his company was a household brand name famous for its smartphones. He built a multibillion-dollar brand almost overnight, and my friend had a net worth in the hundreds of millions. It's one thing to hear about Jeff Bezos and Bill Gates. It's another to see someone you personally know become an overnight success. He was thriving in Extremistan. That's where I wanted to be.

I realized that my map of reality could only get me so far. But that map was the whole world as I knew it. How could I redraw my map of the *new* world? I realized I needed a barbell strategy: extremes on both ends. Imagine the two weights connected in the middle. One side of the barbell was conservative financial stability. The other was extreme risk-reward opportunities. I needed to be able to take risks and seek that giant 1 percent success while working from a rock-solid foundation.

I needed answers. I needed a guide for my journey. Who else was questioning the doctrines perpetuated by the government, the academy, and mass media? I researched different groups and organizations that could help me understand reality better. A few groups looked promising, and I started exploring them.

Before, I would have dismissed those groups as tinfoil-hat conspiracy theorists. But I realized that the mainstream collective did not accurately describe reality. They just wanted us all to believe their doctrines. Jordan Hall calls the mainstream collective the Blue Church—institutions who hold actual and influential power, hard and soft power respectively.[1] They're the ones telling you that the company is your family before throwing you out in the street to line their pockets. During that time, I came across the term GSRRM.

And that's when I realized that the Blue Church uses GSRRM tactics to keep people from questioning their narrative, their map of reality they want us all following so they can retain power. I met Curt Doolittle from the Natural Law Institute online and got my first taste of speaking with someone who truly understood reality. He was the first person I met who documented and showed how, operationally, the Blue Church uses GSRRM tactics.

It was in that online circle I met Noah. He was vocal. He replied to Curt's posts with additional insights and examples of manipulation. I saw that Noah "got it." He became a central figure in the group. And he took on private clients to help them overcome the manipulation at work and in their relationships.

---

[1] Jordan Hall, "Understanding the Blue Church," Medium, March 30, 2017, https://medium.com/deep-code/understanding-the-blue-church-e4781b2bd9b5.

I realized I had come as far as I could on my own to better understand the world. And I needed help to get to the next level. It was the classic hero's journey. I had reluctantly gone on a quest and had reached the threshold. I needed a mentor to help me reach the next stage of my journey. And I wanted Noah to be that mentor.

When I signed up with Noah, he didn't tell me what to believe. He guided me to find my own answers rooted in truth instead of comfortable lies. Good coaching mentors are different from teachers. Teachers tell you, "This is the right answer, and this is the only right way to get that answer." But Noah helped me answer my own questions, solve my own problems, and achieve my own goals. That created true change from within me as opposed to a teacher telling me what to do. He refused to let me become dependent on him but taught me to stand on my own and think for myself. That's what a good coach does.

I'm still on that journey of discovery. I probably will be for as long as I live. Reality is infinitely complex. No one map can document all of reality. But the map I now have offers a better description of reality. My new map has helped me get a better sense of what I want out of life. It's not a prescriptive path like I got from parents or the Blue Church that demands I get a corporate job and jump through the hoops just to please others. I'm now able to seek out my own path. That's an empowering experience.

Through my journey, I learned that it's not enough to want a better life. You must be able to identify and avoid manipulation (or defend against it when avoidance isn't possible) to pursue your own path. I'd been manipulated by so many people into staying in my Mediocristan world with a false sense of security that evaporated the moment my colleagues were shoved out the door. I knew that to be strong, I'd need to make sure I never fell for manipulation again. And Noah showed me how to do that.

This book contains many of the empowering lessons Noah shared with me. I want more people to have the same insights I experienced, to draw a better map of reality and pursue their own path free from manipulation. Noah can get you there, and this book will open your eyes like he opened mine.

GSRRM manipulation tactics pull down a veil in front of your eyes, preventing you from accurately perceiving reality. You can't draw your own map of reality and follow it if you're unable to accurately perceive the world. Manipulation tactics short-circuit your brain, preventing you from reasoning and only allowing you to feel and react based on those feelings.

That's why it's not enough to learn to avoid manipulation. You need to know how to defend against it, to proactively dismantle it and prevent yourself from being snared. This book won't just teach you how to stay safe. It will teach you how to navigate to safety even in the middle of a manipulation minefield.

This book is for anyone who senses something is wrong but can't quite put their finger on the problem. It's for anyone who wants long-term positive outcomes in their life, business, career, and relationships—and who wants those outcomes done ethically as opposed to seeking short-term gain at the expense of others. If you want to succeed without giving up your principles, this is the book for you.

When Noah asked me to read this book, I immediately thought of three groups of people who need it most. If you're a business owner who truly cares about the well-being of your people and your organization and who wants to build a well-functioning, healthy organization for the long term. If you work in an organization and care about building a healthy work environment for yourself and your team. And if you work with people solving their problems, such as a lawyer, therapist, or public servant. All three of these situations demand you read this book. You must understand how to tear out manipulation by the root and keep yourself and your environment honest and free.

Other manipulation books are dry and feel like you're reading a psychology textbook. You're going to enjoy the way this book is written because Noah breaks down a complicated topic into plain, everyday language anyone can read, understand, and share. It's all based on years of experience coaching victims *and perpetrators* of manipulation. Noah has uniquely coached both sides of manipulation because perpetrators often started as victims themselves. Noah coaches manipulators to be better human beings, to realize how their streak of manipulation poisoned their own well and made their lives miserable.

My only regret on my hero's journey is that I wish I had found Noah sooner. He would have saved me a lot of confusion, struggle, and heartache. By reading this book, you're getting the bootstrap I wish I had when I started out. Your journey will be even stronger for it.

Finally, this book includes a lot of useful stories as examples. But this book goes beyond stories. It's a manual on how to avoid and defend against manipulation. By the time you're done reading it, you'll know how to enter any situation and protect yourself. You'll command respect. Manipulators will know they can't mess with you anymore. That will give you the leverage to build a life based on honesty, integrity, and principles.

I'm glad you're reading this book. It means you'll heal from whatever lies you've been taught to believe in. If, like me, you sense something is wrong in reality, and if you want to gain a better understanding, or if you are unsatisfied with how your life is going and you want to be a better version of yourself, Noah is the guide to help you through this. He can help you liberate yourself from years of manipulation that have been programmed into you without you even realizing it. You're on your own hero's journey and need a hero's mentor. Noah is that mentor.

I highly recommend you read his book and then reach out to him. He can help you the way he's helped me. I believe that with all my heart.

For now, enjoy this book. You'll gain great insights that will boost your immunity to manipulation. And you'll cross over from a life of control to a life of ful-fillment. That will make all the difference. Noah will get you where you need to be.

Good luck on your journey.

Francis Zhou
www.franciszhou.com

CHAPTER 1

ARE YOU BEING MANIPULATED?

A re you being manipulated?

Maybe there is dread in the pit of your stomach. But you're not sure. So you're left wondering, *What if someone is taking advantage of me, and I'm letting them?*

People would only buy a book called *How to Stop Getting Bullied* if someone was bullying them. And you bought a book called *Become Immune to Manipulation.* Odds are good you've been manipulated in the past. That means you had a blind spot. If you haven't uncovered that blind spot, you're at risk of being manipulated again. Maybe someone is even manipulating you right now, and you know it —but you can't figure out how to break free.

The ugly truth about modern life is that manipulation is a constant. We all know there are people and corporations targeting us with manipulation. No matter how smart you are, how rich you are, or how successful you are, you must be on alert. That's probably why you picked up this book.

After all, the whole world has reasons to manipulate us. Political candidates promise anything to get your vote. They don't really care about you or your problems. Corporate propaganda sells you junk food to maximize profits at your expense, hoping you have kids before you die so they can continue marketing to an eternal customer base. Even the big stuff we buy for ourselves comes with manipulation. Do you really need *that* fancy a car or *that* big a house? How many things do you own right now that you regret?

Manipulation can even come from those who should be protecting us: our spouse, our parents, or our child. Maybe you suspect someone you know personally is exploiting you, and you want to know what you can do about it.

But how do you know if someone is really manipulating you or if you're just feeling oversensitive because you've been burned by past experiences? There's a simple test to tell the difference. If you find yourself thinking, *I just have to accept what they are saying even though I think it's probably not true*, you are being manipulated. You know you are being manipulated if you feel like you have to accept something wrong or unreasonable. That relationship is not built on trust. It's built on your silence.

Run that test right now on the relationship that prompted you to read this book. If the result makes you cringe, then you bought the right guide.

But knowing we're being manipulated doesn't necessarily make it easier to resist. Why don't we leave manipulative romances, friendships, jobs, transactions, and other situations? When our corporate job forces us to pretend we're part of a family, why don't we speak up and walk out?

Because manipulation happens when the manipulator believes they've got leverage. Something keeps us from speaking up and walking out, and they count on that. Because we feel powerless, we stay stuck in these situations for too long. We have no tool set to detect and confirm we are being manipulated—and know when to walk away when the manipulation has gone too far. Where do we draw the line? We usually only leave when the pain is intolerable. By that point, the maximum damage is already done.

In a romantic relationship, because we've invested so many resources, we feel we've wasted the best we had to offer. We wish desperately for a way to redeem the situation. This is the sunk-cost fallacy and tends to hurt smarter people more because they are more aware of their losses. The manipulator often senses this and sweetens the relationship to keep you trapped.

We rely on our feelings to help manage being manipulated. But acting on feelings like trust, camaraderie, and loyalty is the worst way to respond to manipulation. You burn out fast, and soon you fear you'll never trust anyone ever again.

If you're wondering how I can possibly describe your struggles so clearly, it's because I've lived them myself. And I've watched too many other people suffer from chronic manipulation just like this.

How It Feels to Be Manipulated

I'm a relationship and business coach. People hire a coach like me when something is going wrong in their life, and they can't figure out what to do. That something usually involves manipulation, so I've seen a lot of truly ugly situations.

I once had a client—I'll call him Marco—who came to me after he lost $150,000 in six months to a charismatic manipulator, Pete. First $100,000, then $50,000. It started with a get-rich-quick scheme from someone Marco trusted. "Hey, I found this great way to invest—options trading. It's guaranteed money." Marco isn't an idiot. He is, quite honestly, a naturally skeptical person who prides himself on not falling for scams or schemes.

If anyone could have avoided manipulation to this degree, it should have been Marco.

But Pete was his friend. He'd always seemed trustworthy. Entrepreneurial. Risk taking. Exciting. So Marco hired his buddy as his money manager. And his account rose 30 percent in value. In a week. Then three weeks later, it crashed. To almost zero. Marco checked his balance and saw a slim 3 percent left of the total, from $100,000 down to $3,000.

Marco was desperate to find out what had happened. How could it turn this bad in such a short time? Pete had promised him huge returns. Suddenly, it was hard to reach the guy. When Marco finally did secure a meeting, Pete made it all about himself. "I feel terrible. What a rare stroke of bad luck. Why did this have to happen to *me*? I am so depressed. I can't even get out of bed anymore."

My client, like all kind-hearted people, wanted to help his friend. Marco thought, *If only I could help this person get his life back in order*. Lo and behold, Pete came back with a way he could help.

"I figured this out. Let's start a trading business together, and we'll use each other's strengths." So they ran this for a month. And it worked. Pete even slept over at my client's house so they could get up and start working at six in the morning when the markets opened. Things seemed great. Meanwhile, Pete roped in another friend, a man named Alexei whom Marco hadn't met, and they each put in $50,000 to start a real company.

Marco was an organized person, so of course he kept records of all his financial dealings from day one. Bringing in another partner turned the dial of Marco's systemization instinct way up, and he kept track of every detail. And Pete took it as a personal attack, asking, "Don't you trust me? Don't you trust my friend?" over and over until my client stopped paying such close attention. When Marco raised doubts about certain decisions, he was undermined. "You don't know anything about this industry. Trust me, I know what I'm doing," Pete would say.

The new three-partner dynamic soon normalized. Marco backed off. Until suddenly, things went south. Account values fell. Trades got riskier and riskier. And Pete got paranoid, accusing Marco of stealing his trade secrets. Or perhaps he was using this as an excuse to cover for the money he had lost. Pete played the victim to other investors they had met, using gossip to rally his and Alexei's social circles against Marco, who suddenly "couldn't be trusted."

At first, the trading business collapsed slowly, then all at once. And that was that. Marco had lost everything he'd put into it.

When Marco found me through Twitter one day, we first performed an autopsy on the dead partnership. In retrospect, the charismatic business partner had an unusual sensitivity to manipulation. Pete grew up with a single mom who had manipulated him since birth, so he became overly sensitive about being lied to. Marco never lied to him, but Pete accused him anyway. Marco realized the guy had gained his sympathy in the same way. Pete had told my client about former business partners in another country who made him a victim—then he praised my client to gain his trust and sympathy.

This should have been a heads-up that Pete would also gossip about my client—which he did, to the third partner, Alexei, and to many others. And then, when the wind shifted, Pete tried to make up with Marco by gossiping about Alexei. This poisoned Marco and Alexei's relationship. Who could believe who?

When the two partners stopped responding to Pete's manipulation tactics, the guy dropped off the map. He disappeared. To find someone else to spin his story to, most likely.

A year later, Alexei's wife had had enough of trying to rebuild the family's savings all by herself. She called Marco to check in and figure out what on earth had happened. Only then did they realize how badly they'd all been manipulated.

Nobody wants to admit they were manipulated. There is great shame found in admitting gullibility. Nobody wants to be the fool.

And manipulators know that.

Which is why it works.

Why Manipulation Worked on Me (And How I Got Free)

So how did I come to coach clients through the aftermath of manipulation? How can I claim to be an expert at helping people safeguard themselves from ever being manipulated again? And how can I spot manipulators long before they unleash a scheme?

Because I, too, was manipulated. When I finally woke up to the lies I'd been living in, I immersed myself in figuring out what went wrong. I studied everything I could find on manipulation. I became an expert in manipulation secrets. And it was a brutal journey.

The worst lie I grew up believing was that I was supposed to be a "Nice Guy." That's what I was taught by childhood authorities. In school they told us, "Shut up, keep your head down, and get along." Intelligence was not praised. The only metric that mattered was memorizing correct answers and parroting them on command.

Children's education at church was no better. Their rules were endless and made even less sense. Don't look threatening. Accept responsibility for doing unpaid work. If you ever say no to any request, you're selfish at best and unholy at worst. If you don't use your talents to serve the church, God will take them away.

It didn't even stop at home. The media and my own extended family bombarded me with manipulative propaganda. I was accused of being selfish with trendy messages. "It's selfish to want a spouse and children. Don't you know the earth is overpopulated?" And there was shame for wanting what our grandparents took for granted. "If you grow a beard, nobody will take you seriously. You'll look unprofessional. You'll look like a terrorist."

When I matured enough to understand the sermons, I found the messages even worse. Half the older adults in leadership told us impressionable youth things like, "If you don't work with your hands, you're lazy." The other half said, "If you have to work with your hands, you're stupid."

It wasn't enough to conform on the outside. Even our internal feelings were under constant attack. We weren't allowed to get angry about anything, no matter how badly we were treated. "Nice guys don't get angry." No matter that plenty of people in the Bible got mad, and it was righteous fury that drove them to seek justice. But the church overemphasized docile, sheeplike behavior among the members. "Turn the other cheek" became code for "Accept every slap without even trying to stop the abuse."

Everything was "damned if I do, damned if I don't." It was psychological judo, using my own energy against me. People who are off balance are easy to manipulate and get forced into submission. You want the pain to end, so you accept their version of the truth and don't ask questions.

I wasn't a good sheep. I asked questions anyway. And I got my wrists slapped. A lot.

Then my first child was born. I promised myself I would never manipulate my son. Even as I was still being manipulated, I knew I didn't want to pass that on to him. I *could not* pass everything wrong in my life on to him. I'd look in the mirror after realizing another layer of my own exploitation and tell myself, "I am not raising a sheep."

But I didn't know how. I had the desire, but no tools.

Then, through online circles and social media, I came across the work of Curt Doolittle. Curt described a manipulation strategy that short-circuits our critical thinking through undermining and reputation destruction. He called it "(G)ossiping, (S)haming, (R)allying, (R)idicule, (M)oralizing, (P)sychologizing, (U)ndermining, (R)eputation destruction, and saving (F)ace or consent," or GSRRM.[2]

Suddenly, everything made sense. Studying Doolittle's work helped me form a coherent worldview and understand the source of my cognitive dissonance. I realized I had been manipulating myself on behalf of my abusers! Then I realized that if I could make it impossible to manipulate myself, I could also make it impossible for anyone else to manipulate me. Because no one can be

---

[2] Curt Doolittle, "What Does GSRM Stand For?" The Natural Law Institute, February 23, 2019, https://propertarianinstitute. com/2019/02/23/definition-gsrm-or-gsrrm/.

manipulated without their own consent. That's right—consent is required for manipulation to proceed. So why we consent? Often, it's out of habit.

Everything in my life improved after I stopped allowing manipulation. In our social media cancel culture, I'm doing just fine. I'm cancel-proof. My son is growing up rational and strong for his age. He, too, can see through manipulation. We discuss it and examine propaganda with critical thinking so he learns to dissect things on his own.

When you refuse to be manipulated, people notice. Manipulators notice, of course, but also the vast majority of people who are sick of being exploited notice. People started asking me how I was doing this, speaking my mind honestly online without getting banned, and I offered to help them.

It was a short road from reading Doolittle to coaching people to stop being manipulated. Because once you see the truth, you see it everywhere you look. When a client hires me, I can see not only the way they're being manipulated by others but also the way they're manipulating themselves.

The demand for this knowledge is enormous. No one wants to be manipulated. It was unsustainable to do all this teaching for free, so I started charging to support myself and my family. Soon it became frustrating to only coach one-on-one because my waiting list swelled, and I couldn't help everyone who wanted to work with me.

That's why I wrote this book. I've compiled my entire knowledge base about resisting all forms of manipulation so you can become immune, just like my clients. If you're tired of being exploited, opening this book was the best thing you could have done. Here's what you're going to get out of reading it.

How This Book Immunizes You against Manipulation

This book is built on one idea: You cannot be manipulated without your consent. Every chapter of this book will help you intentionally withdraw all consent to being manipulated. By the end, you'll be a fortress against exploitation, and you'll be able to spot manipulators from a mile away.

This book is like martial arts for your mind, heart, and soul. It's also armor to protect you from any attempted manipulation attacks you might face.

We already take these precautions with our physical bodies. We learn to protect ourselves from attackers. We buckle up before we hit the road. Why not do the same for our minds? And manipulation's toll can be so much worse. We pay with our joy, our hope, and our humanity. People who face constant manipulation are overcome with addictions, self-medication to dull the pain of not being able to protect themselves. Even if they quit, they feel miserable, withdraw, and fall short of their full potential. Some even turn into manipulators themselves.

Manipulation will always exist. Martial arts and seat belts don't prevent beatings or car wrecks; they help protect you from the damage. They give you a defense against reality. The same is true of this book. You'll learn everything you need to defend yourself from harm—no matter what manipulation gets thrown at you. Manipulation will always exist. And it will be constantly thrown at you. But this book shows how you can actively identify and defend against them.

You might wonder why I want to share all these secrets with you instead of keeping them to myself. It's a fair question in a world full of exploitation. And I've got some specific objectives in mind when I teach people what I know.

First of all, I aim to drastically reduce the effectiveness of manipulation and lies on the general public. That keeps everyone better protected. I also hope this book raises the agency of the public by inoculating them to the typical lies and manipulation tactics used against them.

Second, I want to force manipulators and liars out into the open, expose their game, and require them to deal honestly with others. When everyone can spot their deceptions, they'll have no more victims. This will end the ugly cycle. The most natural manipulators were often manipulated as young children by their parents. A manipulation-free world is better for everyone. By educating everyone about these dangers, I can reduce the amount of manipulation in the world.

In more clinical terms, I'm delivering a society-wide dose of a social antiparasitic vaccination.

Once you become immune to manipulation, everything changes. You'll stop tolerating exploitation. That means you'll enjoy better relationships with your family and kids because those relationships will be purged of dishonesty and instead will rely on true connection and mutual fulfillment.

You'll also be able to trust people again. That happens when you can see through every deception, and you know who has your best interests in mind—and who's out to take advantage of you. You'll finally be able to see who your real friends are.

Learning to counter manipulation will also force bad actors to treat you better. Manipulators will switch tactics and be nice to you when they realize their ugly ways don't work because they're cowards at heart and want to minimize their own friction, even at your expense. Then they'll run the other way to get away from you. That means your life is about to become much less stressful.

Becoming a fortress against deception makes you powerful. It makes people respect you. Soon other people trust you to watch over them and protect them from manipulators in the world.

There are also the more mundane but equally exciting benefits. You'll pay less for cars, houses, and other higher-priced items and services. You'll avoid scams. You'll ask for the raise you always wanted. All this adds up to a lot more money in your pocket.

More freedom, more respect, and more money. Doesn't that sound good?

The End of Manipulation

Now you know why manipulation is such a problem. But to be honest, haven't you always known? Maybe you didn't put it into words, but manipulation has really made your life suck on occasion. And it's probably been responsible for the worst memories you hold.

The first step to protecting yourself is education. We're going to study why, when, and how manipulation is used against you—in the same way that virologists first study how a virus attacks your immune system. The cure comes only after they understand the problems that the virus creates.

Manipulation is a virus. It's also psychological warfare on a personal scale. And I'm preparing you for battle.

The famous strategist Sun Tzu wrote, "Know thy enemy." Manipulators are everyone's enemy, and it's time to learn about why they've been so effective at hurting you.

CHAPTER 2

A BRIEF HISTORY OF MANIPULATION

Remember the Kin? The keyboard slider phone was Microsoft's first attempt at a branded smartphone. Mobile device consumers were well acquainted with Windows Mobile when the Kin project started in 2008. Before this project, Microsoft rarely ventured into creating hardware, being a software company that let others do technology design and manufacturing. Kin represented a big leap of faith, not just designing, building, and selling a product but an entirely new brand at that. This would be the Microsoft answer to the iPhone, released by Apple in 2007. AT&T had an exclusive contract with Apple at the time, and Verizon executives saw the Kin as their golden opportunity to offer their customers a true iPhone alternative, backed by a well-established heavyweight in the high tech industry.

Microsoft poured more than $2 billion, two years, and millions of man hours into getting it done. Everything seemed set up for success. But no one accounted for the factor that ruins so many projects, relationships, and dreams: manipulation.

How do I know? Because I coached one of the engineers who was part of the Kin team from the start to the end. My client—we'll call him Dennis—was working in a mid-level Microsoft leadership position when he received an offer to join the team that was going to launch a Microsoft smartphone. They'd build the hardware themselves and adapt the software from the Windows Mobile (WinMo) team, a separate division within Microsoft with its own governance structure.

Why create the Microsoft phone? Because the iPhone was eating WinMo's lunch. That sank the WinMo team's stars in upper management's eyes, which helped the Kin business development (hereafter "bizdev") team sell company leadership on the need for a new Microsoft phone that would rival the iPhone. You see, the business development leadership at that time could sell sandals in winter. This project shift was a major reassignment for the software developers who already had their own work to do. And Microsoft teams weren't used to designing mobile hardware. Still, the pairing seemed perfect.

At the start of the project, the Kin team was a select crew, relatively few in number but dedicated to the challenges. Dennis watched the team grow from twenty to five hundred. Kin and WinMo were always two distinct teams from the beginning, with some "sibling rivalry" between them. The goal was to unite their two products into one excellent smartphone.

In 2009, one year into Kin development, Dennis saw a dark turn. He now believes that Microsoft's business development leadership oversold the phone to upper company management and to Verizon. They promised features and functions without understanding their technical feasibility. When they brought those requirements to engineering, they simply said, "Make this work. Because we need you to."

Engineering did the best they could. But there were other problems. The team was supposed to build on the Windows Mobile operating system the WinMO team had already developed. But the WinMO team had political disagreements with the Kin team and refused to share, so the Kin team had to forge their own path. Which meant the Kin team now needed to build the entire stack from the ground up, with less than half the engineering staff WinMo team had, in addition to designing the hardware.

But it was too late to back out. Microsoft had already signed a deal with Verizon to release this phone on their network. It needed to happen one way or another.

Meanwhile, the iPhone was solidifying its market dominance. The bizdev folks knew the iPhone's capabilities but had talked themselves into believing "We are building this for a different persona, a different audience. Hence, we don't need to compete with iPhone feature by feature." The Kin needed to be on par with the iPhone, but better, and with only two years to build everything from scratch. One year had already passed, yet the project was nowhere near the halfway point.

That's when, according to Dennis, bizdev leadership began to distort reality. They couldn't accept that they'd overpromised and misunderstood engineering's capabilities, so they got defensive. Problems became the engineering team's fault. Concerns were rejected. In response to criticism about feature decisions, bizdev told engineering, "We're not building this for you. You're not our target market." That's the wrong thing to tell your design team who's creating the product you have to market.

Dennis shared one distinct memory that left a deep impression on him. After a planning meeting about the Kin phone camera, Dennis told bizdev, "With the camera specs you want and time we've been given, we're not going to meet the quality level expected. What you want is on par with a three-thousand-dollar professional DSLR. It's just impossible for the phone form factor with the current level of technology, not to mention the price point." A bizdev manager said, "That's simply not good enough. You just gotta work harder." It was all the engineering team's fault for not knowing how to create inexpensive replicas of top-line equipment on the fly.

The engineering team began whispering the harsh truth to each other: "We have to ship this phone in a year. The software is *crawling*. This isn't going to happen." No one believed the Kin would be competitive against the iPhone. It might not even work.

So the engineering leads got together with bizdev and told them the straight facts. Bizdev's response? "You don't know what you're talking about." Then they launched into a list of requirements they wanted added to the existing prototype. "The iPhone has this, so we need to build it into the Kin," and so on.

It became apparent there was a fundamental disconnect between the business vision and the engineering reality. The engineering team wanted to build something they would actually use. But bizdev envisioned Kin to be a cheaper version of the iPhone and made for the late-teen, early-twenties market—basically a better Sidekick with iPhone capabilities. Meanwhile, Kin bizdev continued to promise Verizon a Microsoft smartphone that would compete with the iPhone. Developed and built in two years. And engineering knew it could not be done.

You are probably recognizing the manipulation in this story. It may even sound like some troubled relationships you've experienced in your own career or personal life. In the relationship dynamic between bizdev and engineering, bizdev was effectively the boss. Every problem was blamed on the subordinate team. "You don't know what you are talking about," was the standard response to concerns. Any unpleasant data that engineering brought to bizdev was first questioned, then summarily dismissed.

Meanwhile, bizdev projected hundreds of millions in revenue in Kin's first year, a billion-dollar business in year two, and skyrocketing profits after that. "I don't think you're going to hit those numbers," Dennis said at a meeting. A bizdev manager replied, "We don't need pessimism at Microsoft."

Truth telling was now taboo, and that was the beginning of the Kin team's downward spiral in morale. From the end of 2008 to the end of 2009, employee motivation sank. Engineering told bizdev it wouldn't work, their concerns were ignored, so they did not put in the best effort they could have. To complicate matters further, Microsoft acquired Danger, Inc., and many good engineers unfamiliar with Microsoft culture were suddenly placed on the Kin project to make up for resource shortfalls, exacerbating issues in collaboration and communication. To add insult to injury, when the Great Recession hit, many of those people were let go.

If you know anything about the Kin, you know how poorly the product sold. We'll discuss that in a moment. Let's focus now on how this corporate project went so wrong. The Microsoft bizdev team used a myriad of manipulation tactics against everyone involved. Those tactics worked in the short term but cost Microsoft a lot in the long run. Microsoft spent $500 million just to acquire Danger, Inc. and invested billions more in the Kin project.

But the raw manipulation perpetrated on the team undercut all their best efforts. The project imploded as a result. Manipulation was to blame.

How Manipulation Ruined Microsoft's First Smartphone

The bizdev team used nine specific manipulation tactics to undermine the Kin project.

Gossiping. When the iPhone came out in 2007, bizdev took that as validation that an integrated hardware and software stack could be a viable business. They looked down on the WinMo team's (apparently failed) software-only strategy: starting years earlier than Apple yet being leapfrogged overnight. So they gossiped about the Windows Mobile team. "Look how bad they're doing; iPhone is eating their lunch. We're doing it right with the Kin." What started off as gossiping about other teams to feel superior turned into gossiping about their own team, too. That destroyed morale.

Shaming. Bizdev shamed engineering. They said things like, "You don't know what you're talking about," and "We're not building this for you." The engineers who were building the phone and software were made to feel like idiots who didn't comprehend bizdev's grand vision.

Rallying. Bizdev solicited multiple allies to speak up in favor of their plans against the engineers. "Our entire team thinks this is going to work." That made the engineers feel like it was everyone else against them. Rallying to solve problems, as if it's a democracy, is a big problem in the corporate world. There are good ways and bad ways to utilize rallying, and when you weaponize it against your own team, you alienate people you should be listening to. The Danger employees, for example, came in to offer help, but when it was clear that Microsoft, which had spent $500 million to acquire their expertise, didn't actually want to hear their advice grounded in reality, there was an ugly power dynamic. Rallying always brings that danger. Pulling together at the expense of some of your own teammates eventually destroys the team mentality.

Ridiculing. This tactic is plain vicious, and we're all familiar with it. "You just don't understand marketing. Let me educate you." It's a brute-force way to tell someone to shut up and stop voicing their opinion. The underlying message is "I don't respect your opinion, and I don't want to hear another word from you." Imagine the effect that has on employees when it comes from their perceived boss or real boss or teammates.

Moralizing. When engineers shared concerns about the product, bizdev sometimes responded like they were holding a religious inquisition. "Are you doubting the entire mission?" was asked in response to doubts about user interface or feature specs, not even the entire project itself. Everyone on the team was initially delighted to be building a first for Microsoft—their own smartphone! Then moral questioning was thrown at the team to silence dissenting voices that raised important questions in good faith. No one could express their concerns without being treated as a saboteur.

Psychologizing. "You can't understand what a teenager wants. We have the market research. We understand our customer persona." Bizdev told engineers to shut up and build the phone they were told to build without complaints because that was the phone customers wanted. They assigned psychological issues to the victims and made them feel they were inferior to the bizdev staff.

Undermining. There were layers of shielding within the project. When engineering raised concerns, they were stopped from traveling up the hierarchy. A woman from bizdev was the first GM, then VP. She was directly in charge of the entire Kin project. She surrounded herself with loyal bizdev employees who hid all bad news from her. When any bad news got through her inner defenses, that woman shielded her boss from hearing about it.

That's why CEO Steve Balmer was kept from hearing any bad news and therefore had every reason to believe Kin was a multibillion-dollar business in the making. If anyone from upper management had walked the halls and listened in, they would have known this project was in trouble. As an aside, some Microsoft leaders do randomly drop by and talk to employees about what's going on. This prevents undermining of communication—and undermining morale and confidence. Too bad they didn't implement this for the Kin project.

Reputation destruction. The executive vice president of that entire division, of which Kin was just a small part, had to resign. That's a crushing end to an otherwise distinguished career. It's hard to get hired anywhere else after presiding over a multibillion-dollar mistake, one ranked among the three worst products Microsoft ever released. But mistakes of this magnitude demand blame, and that blame was placed on the EVP.

Guilt by association spread to everyone who touched the project. Everyone associated with Kin now has to explain to future hiring managers what they worked on at Kin. "Well, you worked on Kin, so you must not be very good." Letting the rest of the blame fall on the engineers is how bizdev protected themselves at the expense of everyone else on the team.

Solving for face or consent. When the program tanked like the engineers warned it would, bizdev went into damage-control mode—not for the company but for themselves. "How can we make ourselves look OK and make everyone agree that we're the good guys in this situation?" The EVP took the full blame. Talking points rolled out to protect the company: "The product was way ahead of its time," and "The market wasn't able to comprehend our value." So the bizdev crew was free to scatter into other projects and other companies as if they'd had nothing to do with the disaster.

• • • •

All these tactics were used to avoid the truth. It's important to remember that manipulation didn't just begin out of the blue. These tactics were present from day one up to the EVP's firing. Manipulation was built into the system from the start.

It can be tempting to use manipulation to get tasks accomplished faster. Manipulation, after all, gets things done. And whipping a horse until it bleeds can make it run faster for a short while. But just like animal abuse, manipulation has no error-correction mechanism. There's no stopping the cart once it's out of control because the horse doesn't trust you anymore. Destroying your relationship through manipulation means the victim won't help fix the disaster they saw coming and tried to warn you about.

Persuasion, the opposite of manipulation, *does* have an error-correction mechanism. We'll talk about persuasion later in this book. For now, let's examine further what Kin teaches us about how we are all susceptible to manipulation.

First is the loss of time. Roughly five hundred people working for two years (one thousand human years) could have been spent building a better product—at least a product that would have survived in the market. Engineering suspected this product was doomed but allowed themselves to be manipulated into believing there might be a miracle. The result for the employees was two years wasted at their peak. And they spent even more time healing from this awful experience and finding new jobs where they'd be appreciated.

The financial fallout was a disgrace. Initial reports informed the team that "Kin is not selling as well as expected." Well, duh! Who'd buy a worthless product after the initial reviews tore it apart? The Kin, supposed to rival the iPhone and rake in billions within two years, was pulled from the store shelves weeks after launch. The damage to Microsoft's relationships with Verizon and retail customers still echoes to this day. Do you know anyone who switched to a Windows Phone?

But a damaged culture was the worst outcome for Microsoft. Their internal teams had to cope with the naked manipulation that sank a promising idea. You can always launch a new product, but you can't attract top talent once you get a reputation for ruining careers.

It might seem natural to blame the bizdev team for the entire outcome. That's not my goal. It wasn't just the bizdev team behind this. They were not deliberately manipulating, nor were they "bad" people. They had to first manipulate themselves. And everyone else had to agree to be manipulated.

Let's dissect how manipulation can happen so easily within companies that seem to have everything lined up.

Why Are People Easy to Manipulate?

Time for some harsh truth—the number-one reason we are so easy to manipulate is that we manipulate ourselves in dozens of little ways every day. Instead of dealing with uncomfortable responsibilities, we stick our head in the sand, pretending we don't have a problem when we actually do. Think back to the last time you felt tired. "I should have gone to sleep earlier last night. So I'll drink coffee and eat sugar to stay awake today." That is self-manipulation. You are not happy with your choices, so you try to make the consequences go away. There's no error correction. The caffeine and sugar are going to mess up your brain chemistry and make it harder to sleep well tonight, creating a perpetual cycle of needing coffee and sugar. But you tell yourself, *It's OK. I need it*. You manipulate yourself.

It's fashionable these days to have painful emotional problems that get "triggered." I'm telling you that this trend is based on manipulating yourself into believing it's OK to never heal. Nobody should have "inner demons." Those are the result of self-manipulation and create a constant cycle that prevents you from becoming the best version of yourself.

Sometimes we manipulate ourselves because it is good for business. Look at pickup artists who teach other men online how to exploit wounded women for sex. Over time, I've seen some of these so-called gurus face the consequences of their actions when they have children, meet a woman they want to marry, or suddenly feel alone. "This advice is my business, but it's wrong. If I stop doing it, I'll stop earning a living." This creates even more moral repugnance for them. And not stopping means they'll never be complete. Worrying about teaching other people wrong information turns into "I will never have an honest, authentic connection with a woman."

That's how self-manipulation creates a living hell. We'll do anything to end that pain. And that makes it easy for other people to manipulate us by pretending they want to help.

Those are all reasons we *continue* to self-manipulate; it gets us short-term results, which are what most of us care about. Then we have long-term and mid-term manipulation, in which we off-load our responsibilities onto third parties. Things didn't go the way we wanted? It's not our fault. We manipulate ourselves into blaming our poor results on others, bad luck, or even God instead of our corrupted decision-making process. We keep putting off facing the truth, justifying ourselves to ourselves. This has a cost. Eventually, we run out of road through bankruptcy, divorce, or a total loss of the trust of others. Everyone knows who we are and wants to stay away from the fires we create.

This happens on a corporate level, too. Microsoft tarnished its reputation with Kin, so people viewed Windows Phone, a later product that was the true competitive answer to the iPhone, with a critical eye. Did you even know they released another branded phone later? That's their consequence for manipulation.

The goal of this book isn't just to teach you to avoid manipulation so you stay isolated. The whole point of protecting yourself is to help you shift from manipulation to authentic connection. Using persuasion instead of manipulation is what builds trust. Again, we'll come back to this later. And we'll differentiate manipulation (win-lose) from persuasion (win-win).

For now, let's talk about the root cause. Where does this self-manipulation tendency come from?

We grew up on manipulation. From our parents, our schools, and a constant avalanche of marketing that never lets up. You might think, *My parents didn't manipulate me*, but you tell yourself that because you haven't figured it out yet. Even good parents have bad days and bad behaviors. They twisted you into acting a certain way with less-than-respectful methods.

Some parents are outright awful. They have kids in order to brag to friends about how good they are. Or they have kids to save a failing marriage or use the children as leverage against their partner. Many kids feel manipulated by their parents, the same way that many wives feel manipulated by their husbands and vice versa. Some men get married only because the other person makes them look or feel good. The marriage is not based on mutual benefit. It's not a trusting partnership. Some women do this, too.

Manipulation exists in such abundance because humans are social creatures. We need group approval. Social exclusion has meant death for most of history because without the "tribe," we cannot survive on our own. And social exclusion still means gene death if no one wants to partner with us. Loss of connection and loss of meaning are still dangerous to the human animal.

We have a surprising lack of defenses against manipulation. We spent the last five thousand years domesticating violence (masculine means of coercion) and mostly ignored manipulation (feminine means of coercion). In this case, masculine does not mean only men or feminine only women. Men and women choose different means based on the situation. It's more an attitude: hard coercion versus soft coercion. Push versus pull. Physical coercion versus psychological coercion.

You might be thinking right now, *I hate manipulating people. I'd feel horrible about doing it.* Excellent. But many people are not like you. And you need to understand the minds out there trying to manipulate you.

Why Do People Manipulate Others?

Because it works great for getting short-term results. Sometimes. Look at developing countries. You travel there as a tourist and have to guard yourself against fraud. There are scams and thieves and lies all around you. They're not looking at cultivating long-term relationships with tourists. They want to milk every dollar they can and cut you loose. Are all people in developing countries like this? Certainly not. But the manipulative individuals stay clustered in areas where tourists will be in the hopes of preying on them. That's how they make a living while tarnishing their nation's reputation and ability to attract productive investment.

Another reason manipulation is popular is that power is addictive, like a drug. Manipulation appeals to people who feel they have no power (even if they do have power). Getting good at manipulation leads to a dark confidence in your ability to get what you want at the expense of others. Your brain learns that it feels good to manipulate.

Some women manipulate men. This is true of sex workers as well as serial divorcees who hunt for rich husbands. But women who use persuasion instead have legitimate power over men because they aren't inflicting harm. Recall the Greek myth of Zeus and Hera. He gets ready to do something stupid, she cooks him a hot meal with tons of wine, and he gets drunk and passes out. When he wakes up, he's annoyed but admits he was about to do something stupid, and she saved him from himself. She didn't harm him through her manipulation but did what was actually best for him long term. That's a lesson on the power of persuasion to achieve a win-win. Contrast that with a man who gets drunk and spends his whole paycheck at the strip club and then feels manipulated when he can't pay his rent. There was harm done that ran counter to the victim's best interests.

Persuasion is about long-term wins with much higher payoffs. Manipulation focuses on a short-term high score with a worse long-term outcome. But keep in mind that both sides must participate in order for manipulation to proceed. One person is just manipulating themselves and creating an opening for the other person to manipulate them.

In game theory, we call manipulation a zero-sum game. It's the Prisoner's Dilemma, in which people have a tendency to end up in mutual-defection situations with worse long-term payoffs. But persuasion is working together so both sides win. This is the current state of our society. All sides are manipulating themselves and others. It's creating the worst long-term outcomes, all done so that a few can make short-term gains and get out before the consequences surface.

Manipulation is profitable for the manipulator. Get-rich-quick schemes only get manipulators rich quick. This is profitable for people who overpromise and under-deliver because they have no value to offer, no win to exchange for a win. When people lack value to trade, they manipulate instead. Then they get out fast before the consequences catch up to them, and you're left hold-ing the bag.

What is Manipulation?

	Process	Gains	Who Wins?	People?	Legacy
Violence	physical coercion	short term	win/lose	objects	fear
Manipulation	social coercion	short term	win/lose	objects	distrust
Persuasion	ethical exchange	long term	win/win	human agents	trust and intimacy

How the Human Mind Works (To Manipulate and Be Manipulated)

Manipulability is built into our biological hardware and software. We have a tripartite (three-part) brain, and manipulation targets two of the parts.

First is the neocortex. This allows for higher thought. Manipulators don't typically target this part of the brain because people tend to recognize the attempts. Manipulators just have to be aware of the neocortex so they don't trigger any of its alarms while they attempt to work on the other two parts.

Second is the mammalian brain. This part focuses on making sure we're part of a group. That makes us feel safe. Threats to the mammalian brain make us feel scared, and that's a powerful form of manipulation. "If you don't join my direct sales company, all these nice people you know won't like you." No one wants to feel left out. Manipulators recognize this.

Last is the lizard brain. This is where your basic impulses and desires come from: food, pleasure, sex. And this is what marketing targets most of all. "If you don't buy our product, you won't get laid." Our lizard brain doesn't want to miss out.

It's crucial that you understand what manipulation does to you. Manipulation is like psychological junk food. It meets the dopamine need to feel an accomplishment. For a moment, we feel like the problem is fixed. Then the consequences hit, and we need something to make us feel better. More manipulation fills that gap, for a while.

The important thing to remember is that you've got "buttons" installed that any manipulator can push.

Those buttons, installed by your parents, teachers, and society in general, exist in the lizard and mammalian brains. And your manipulators can be anyone—parents, siblings, extended family, friends, colleagues, corporations, government agencies, and con artists looking to steal your money.

Some manipulations are obvious. For example, "Accept everyone just the way they are" is society-wide manipulation. But that doesn't work when the other side wants to harm you. Then there are more subtle manipulations, especially ones we learn as kids. "You have to share." Then the IRS comes along when we're adults and forces us to share. And we're used to having our resources taken away, so we don't question increasing taxes. Those buttons work.

What does persuasion look like? It's your parents not yelling at you to take your brother because "you have to" but instead saying, "Take your brother along because he's family. And you're building a bond with your younger sibling that you both will rely on later in life." But most parents go right to manipulation instead. "You *have* to. Because I said so. And I'm the boss." Programing you to believe that your preferences don't matter.

Much of manipulation is based on pain. Mental pain and pleasure are real, which is where we get the mental carrot-and-stick model. And social isolation can feel worse than physical torture. That comes in when major organizations control us by saying, "We're going to shame you so badly no employer will hire you" or "no person will marry you."

It's all about amygdala hijacking. The neocortex came about from generations upon generations of human evolution. The neocortex thinks about future results of current actions, which is counter to what manipulators want. Manipulators throw fearful scenarios at you very quickly to trigger your fight-or-flight response. When the amygdala gets hyped up, you get a cortisol rush and are open to suggestions. Your brain is screaming, "Fix the immediate problem or we won't have a future to worry about." That turns your neocortex off and cuts you down to just your lizard and mammalian brains, which are easier to manipulate.

Even an excess of neutral or conflicting information can overwhelm the brain, leading to a type of paralysis in which the victim stops processing and starts demanding an answer or solution, which the manipulator happily provides.

Extreme examples exist. Brainwashers subject their victims to physical and psychological pain. A drug that numbs the neocortex is the holy grail of manipulation. Such drugs exist. But most manipulators don't require drugs. Your own fear acts as enough of a drug for them to get what they want out of you.

So-called fear porn—intentionally watching disturbing news reports and reading sensationalized accounts of potential disasters and end-of-the-world scenarios—is such an addictive drug that people become hooked on it.

So . . . What Exactly Is Manipulation?

Manipulation is nonreciprocal influence at the cost of another person. It's "I win, you lose." That means you coerce someone else's behavior to suit your desires at their expense. The manipulator is acting as a predator or parasite. A blackmailer is a predator. A prosperity gospel preacher is a parasite.

Manipulation is dishonest. Sometimes that means outright lies while, at other times, the manipulator is lying by omission because they're distracting the victim from thinking about the long-term consequences. Either way, they're distorting reality for their own benefit.

The definition of manipulation expands to include self-manipulation as well. Present you manipulates near-future you at the expense of far-future you.

Understanding manipulation in theory is helpful to define what it is and is not. And you'll need to do more than understand the theory. Seeing manipulation in action empowers us to respond with specific counter-attacks.

We spent this chapter illustrating what manipulation looks like so you could grasp the concept. Now you've got a definition to go with the clear picture.

Both parts are crucial to helping you learn how to defend yourself. Because if you don't know what manipulation is, or if you only know the definition and can't recognize it in the wild, you can't protect yourself. When I've asked people I knew were being manipulated if that's what was happening they said, "No, absolutely not." Then when I asked if they were being shamed, they said yes. I'd tell them, "That's manipulation." That's when it finally clicked.

Now that you know what manipulation looks like and grasp the definition, let's discuss specific tactics manipulators use to control your behavior.

Manipulation Tactics That (Almost Always) Work

We previously mentioned GSRRM, which is an acronym from Curt Doolittle's work examining how manipulation functions. The full definition is "(G)ossiping, (S)haming, (R)allying, (R)idicule, (M)oralizing, (P)sychologizing, (U)ndermining, (R)eputation destruction, and solving for (F)ace or consent."[3]

---

[3] Doolittle, "What Does GSRRM Stand For?"

We've discussed these tactics as they pertained to the Microsoft Kin story, but they can look very different depending on the circumstance. Let's examine each of these specific manipulation tactics so you know what to watch for.

How Framing Sets You Up to Lose

Prior to deploying GSRRM, manipulators will "prime" you so your resistance to the manipulation is softened up. *Influence* author Robert Cialdini calls this "pre-suasion." Another common term for this phenomenon is *framing*. Consider a picture frame. There is a scene or subject in front of you, but your phone's camera frame can only take a picture of a limited area. Framing is therefore a subtractive act—it's what you choose to portray as your version of reality, eliminating everything else.

Framing, pre-suading, priming—whatever we call it—is a technique that drags you into the manipulator's reality. The starting point of manipulation isn't GSRRM, but it does leave you vulnerable to soft coercion. The emotional battleground has been chosen, and not by you.

Bringing other people into your world is not inherently unethical. It becomes unethical when it's used to weaken your agency so it's easier for the manipulator to win and you to lose. It's about control. And dishonesty gives the liar power over those who don't know the truth, which is why manipulative, unethical framing distorts the facts. Lying by omission is one example.

You may have seen the meme depicting a dog biting a sheep's neck in one frame.[4] It looks like the dog is eating the poor, helpless sheep alive. Zoom out—widen the frame—and you see the dog pulling the sheep from raging rapids, saving its life. Good boy.

You will always be the bad guy when the wrong person tells your story.

---

[4] Astra Sheepdog Centre, Facebook photo, September 28, 2021, https://m.facebook.com/astrasheepdogcentre/photos /a.407096049353413/4504229992973311/?type=3&source=48.

Trials in which important evidence is kept out of court, activists who open their arguments by calling their opponents racist or sexist, and scientific studies funded by special interest groups are all examples of manipulative framing. If you're the manipulator's target, you're already playing with a handicap. Then along come GSRRM tactics, and they work like a charm. Here they are.

The 9 GSRRM Tactics Manipulators Use

Gossiping

Sharing details or spreading rumors about someone for malicious purposes. The most classic examples are high school girls spreading rumors about people outside their clique. Fake reviews on Amazon are a modern method of gossip that can affect a business or entrepreneur.

Shaming

Cutting someone down with pressure. You might remind them of past mistakes that make them feel inadequate for making present-day decisions. Or you embarrass them in front of others so they stop resisting.

Rallying

Gathering support among the majority to silence or place pressure on the minority. Abusive parents do this when they say, "None of your siblings have a problem with how I'm acting. You're the only one with a problem." This tactic isolates you even from non-manipulators and makes you feel alone.

Ridiculing

Good old-fashioned insults. You make the target feel so small and so disrespected that they stop struggling. Scummy talent agents use this on clients when they say, "You're too stupid to do this on your own. I've done all the real work. You have no clue how to do anything without me."

Moralizing

Making the victim's objection into a moral issue. A sleazy boyfriend pressuring his girlfriend into sex might say, "Don't you love me?" A cult might ask its hesitant member, "Don't you want to make God happy?"

Psychologizing

Claiming that a person is "crazy" (or has mental or memory defects) for thinking and behaving differently from the manipulator. This includes "gaslighting."

When psychologizing, the manipulator gets into the victim's head or demonstrates that they can get into someone else's head. "I know what people are thinking, and you don't. You have to listen to me." A mother manipulating her child might say, "I have to make all your decisions for you because you've got that diagnosis and that means you're helpless without me. I'm the only one who's smart enough to decide for you."

Reputation Destroying

Shifting blame from the manipulator to the victim. They're never responsible for the long-term consequences of the manipulation. Abusive parents might blame their kids for having mental problems in adulthood by saying, "You're an adult now. Trauma doesn't matter. It's not my fault you're struggling. Take responsibility for yourself."

Undermining

Undermining happens when manipulators create layers of protection to shield the truth of their manipulations. This is one of the most popular manipulation tactics in modern life, so we will examine it in detail.

One of the most common methods of undermining is changing the definition of a term. As people increasingly rely on the internet to help them determine what is and is not true, editing the internet means editing reality. Only information workers are capable of doing this, not carpenters, plumbers, engineers, et cetera. Information workers are the ones who shape the collective sense of truth, for good or for bad.

They do this by changing the meanings of words and descriptions of events. *Anti-vaxxer* used to mean someone who objected to all vaccines, then it became a pejorative against moms who worry about vaccine safety. Now it's used to describe anyone who objects to any vaccine at all, regardless of its safety record. And right now, information workers are fighting over the definition of *woman*. Is it about more than reproductive organs? Is the ability to give birth part of the definition? Is it about the pairs of chromosomes someone is born with? Depending who you ask, you'll get a different answer.

Changing the descriptions of events is even worse. Stealth editing on Wikipedia can erase facts and create an alternate timeline that didn't happen. Those events can then be used as justification for future decisions.

Even if they don't change events, they can seed lies into our world. Information workers do this with sensational headlines that contradict the content. The story says one thing, and you want to read the truth, but you can't see it any other way but to click on their misleading headline and give them attention. And most people don't even read the stories. They rely on the headlines to be factual and react from there. It's the same way political manipulators always show the opposing candidate in an embarrassing pose and their own candidate in the best light. Position the information to *look* bad, and people will assume it *is* bad. Remember that the next time you hear about a "controversial" public figure, "settled science," or "mostly peaceful" protests. Manipulators are attempting to undermine your understanding of reality itself.

If the undermining fails, and they get called out, they deny it all. This is also called gaslighting. "I never said that. Are you crazy? You might be. And you are." They erase the old headlines and articles and change Wikipedia entries so you can't find the truth. The only thing that exists is their endless new "truth" to support their current narrative. In the novel *1984*, George Orwell calls these manipulators the "Ministry of Truth"—a fitting term.

The goal of all this is to shift expectations and change the rules. They bludgeon you down with false definitions and things that never happened to make you agree to what they want. When you're exhausted, you give in. It's like a pickup artist insulting a woman in the hopes she'll sleep with him. "You think you're a ten? Nope. Ugly. Now sleep with me." In this case, it's "You're an anti-vaxxer, and your social group abuses women. You're evil. Donate money to my cause, and I won't point it out anymore."

Solving for Face or Consent

Solving for face or consent (versus the truth) is the final objective of all previous tactics. Solving is when a manipulator tries to look like the good guy (or the victim) to save face at the victim's expense. They cover themselves with plausible deniability and blame the fall guy for everything. An abusive female partner who pushed her male partner to the edge and beat him up psychologically until he fought back can use his fighting back as proof that he abused her. Then she pitches that false abuse to make herself look like a victim. That, in turn, creates situations for her to manipulate more people who rush to her aid. This might remind you of the Johnny Depp and

Amber Heard case.[5] She gaslit potentially millions of Johnny Depp's own fans into believing he was a domestic abuser. Meanwhile, she was the perpetrator all along.

Often, manipulators resort to solving for face when someone they know catches them in a lie. As the truth finally comes out, the manipulator spins one story after another, casting themselves as a victim who was doing the best they could. In child abuse cases involving stepfathers or boyfriends and underage children, often the mother of the victim, afraid of getting embarrassed, losing her new man, and causing additional strife with the child's father, decides instead to manipulate the child into silence. This is the extent to which manipulators will try to solve for face—they will keep their own family under the same roof as a sexual predator.

If the manipulator is unable to make themselves look good and the other party look bad, they try to get the victim's consent for further manipulation. If a manipulator can't save face or get your consent, surrender, or forced agreement, then they failed to manipulate you.

---

[5] Maria Puente, "Johnny Depp Scores Big Win over Amber Heard as Judge Rejects Her Bid to Throw Out His Defamation Suit," *USA Today*, August 17, 2021, https://www.usatoday.com/story/entertainment/celebrities/2021/08/17/johnny-depp-scores-win-over-amber-heard-virginia-defamation-suit/8171254002/.

The Purpose of Psychological Coercion

The goal of manipulation is to gain something at the expense of another person. It's coercing consent by omitting truth.

Manipulation is not always about money. It can be about power or approval the manipulator didn't earn or doesn't deserve. That includes sex, respect, fame, and social status.

Elizabeth Holmes is a famous example of a master manipulator.[6] She misled patients, doctors, and investors about Theranos's blood-testing technology. Through the leader, an entire organization and its shareholders got manipulated.

Bernie Madoff's story is another example.[7] He ran the largest Ponzi scheme in history through his hedge fund. He used many of the above tactics to manipulate

---

[6] Avery Hartmans and Sarah Jackson, "The Rise and Fall of Elizabeth Holmes, the Former Theranos CEO Found Guilty of Wire Fraud and Conspiracy Who Is the Subject of the New Hulu Series 'The Dropout,'" *Business Insider*, last revised March 3, 2022, https://www.businessinsider.com/theranos-founder-ceo-elizabeth-holmes-life-story-bio-2018-4#inspired-by-her-great-great-grandfather-christian-holmes-a-surgeon-holmes-decided-she-wanted-to-go-into-medicine-but-she-discovered-early-on-that-she-was-terrified-of-needles-later-she-said-this-influenced-her-to-start-theranos-7.

[7] Adam Hayes, "Bernie Madoff," Investopedia, last revised April 30, 2021, https://www.investopedia.com/terms/b/bernard-madoff.asp.

well-to-do New York Jews—his own ethnic and religious community!—into giving up their family wealth. Over five hundred of his victims wrote to the judge to request that he not be allowed to leave prison at the end of his sentence. That's how deeply he wounded the people he manipulated.

Look at multilevel marketing. This is also called a pyramid scheme. They use every GSRRM tactic as the business model to get people to sign up. Try to get out and you get pulled back in. The fuzzy math used to promise you great rewards is the worst part. And the people inside say, "I thought we were friends. Just come hear the pitch. You don't have to buy anything." This is how they move you deeper into the trap. The best manipulators target their own communities and try to look, speak, and act like their targets—wolves in sheep's clothing. Some communities have no way to deal with a hardcore manipulator and are totally helpless.

That's not you. Not anymore. This book will help you defend yourself from predators.

To Defend Against Manipulation, Understand It

Manipulation happens every day. You need to understand it to defend yourself and those you love. As frightening as it sounds, with manipulators constantly seeking to take what you have, you don't need to be afraid because they can't take anything from you that you don't allow them to take. Your consent is required. To protect yourself, you need to learn how to withdraw consent to be manipulated. And I'm going to teach you how.

CHAPTER 3

THE TRUE COST OF MANIPULATION

David hired me to help him be more authentic. Here's how that went.

First, you must understand David. He's a great guy. When he signed up for my coaching, his biggest concern was how to get promoted. "How can I be more authentic in my career?" David asked me. "What and how much should I share with the people at work? They promote people they like, and they can't like me if they don't know me."

But shortly after David hired me, his employer was acquired by a multinational corporation. This changed everything about David's company. Before, they'd been a crew of high-IQ individuals run on logic and functionality. What worked best became the rule. Honest feedback and useful criticism were valued because they made things run even more smoothly. Every employee had thick skin and spoke up when problems arose.

Now, standardization was coming. Individual expression was about to be eliminated. Those high-IQ individuals doing the programming were being forced to work in an inefficient environment tailored to average employees from the general population. That meant David was losing the authenticity we'd been working to build. When new, low-performing employees were hired, he could no longer speak up. In the corporate world, objective feedback is dismissed in favor of feelings.

Meanwhile, company leadership—from both the acquiring company and the acquired company—promised that the merger would empower the business to scale to untold shareholder profits. Scaling to the top of any industry is hard, even when your company is run by and hires only geniuses. Yet David's employer had openly committed to doing the opposite.

Each team of geniuses, David's included, was assigned new, nontechnical employees—none of whom matched the competence of the original team members. It was like shoving an average person into a Special Forces team for political reasons while the other Special Forces members think, *This guy is going to get us killed.*

This downgrading of competency meant company meetings had to be tailored to those who were least familiar with high-tech software development. The thing is, only 1 to 2 percent of the entire population can work in this challenging industry. If the company wanted to maintain their previous quality and output, they did not have room for low- or middle-range performers.

Upper management didn't know what to do. Now that the company had been acquired, they weren't in control anymore. Their employees used to be free to point out upper management's mistakes because those leaders were already critical of themselves. But many in the new corporation weren't used to that environment. So problems arose, and no one could talk about them. Soon everything was over budget and late.

People from David's original company were whispering to each other, "Why did they even acquire our company?" It became apparent David's company had looked like a tremendous opportunity to either resell or create a golden parachute for the people behind the acquisition.

In actuality, the acquisition was a disaster for both groups. David's company went from a "product launch" focus to a "social good" focus. The corporation hired social changemakers, not engineers. Everything became about identity instead of capability. Feedback was silenced to protect feelings. David's company went from a software company to a low-performer babysitting service. Who would want to stay and watch their career grow stagnant?

The guys in their fifties and sixties from the original company figured they'd hang around for a few more years until retirement. But the young top performers left once it got unbearable. Most members of middle and upper management accepted buyouts and left to form a direct competitor to the existing corporation. They took many of the best former employees with them. They instituted the old policies and started eating up a new market share as the corporation's efforts crumbled. One upper-management member was recruiting within the corporation—tapping people on the shoulder and saying, "You might want to get out; the ship's going down."

David's desire to be authentic and get promoted shifted to protecting himself from the extreme manipulation in his workplace. Instead of enhancing his career, he wanted to find a new job.

Spot the Manipulation

In this situation, the manipulation was not a secret. Everyone in the original company knew what was going on.

New rules were put in place that worked against common sense. Speaking up could get someone fired. Complaints like "This person does not belong on the team" would be met with "That's not nice. You're being sexist and racist." Employees were shamed and moralized when they questioned policies being driven by social change instead of efficiency. "You're just a bad person for opposing this," the new leaders would say. Yes, in those exact words.

The original team had a strong spirit, but after the acquisition, everyone stopped caring. They shut up. Even those who stayed didn't care anymore. The purpose for hard work was gone. Why work yourself to exhaustion for people who don't care about you or the product? Put in the minimal effort, get your paycheck, and go home.

The new corporate leaders also blamed the original team members for the lack of growth because of their minimum-competency hires. When things didn't go well they said, "You aren't helping them." And they psychologized the original team members: "You have no social skills to work with people."

It went from a logical environment to an emotionally sensitive one. Feelings were all that mattered: the feelings of the protected social groups, that is.

The Costs of Manipulation

You might read the above story and think, "Why would anyone do this? Why destroy an expensive acquisition for feelings?"

That's what manipulation does. It disregards the long-term benefits of healthy behavior to prioritize the short-term rewards of unhealthy behavior. Manipulation accomplished the corporation's immediate goals regarding feelings at the cost of their long-term financial goals.

Let's talk about the types of cost that manipulation can bring to organizations, groups, and individuals.

Business Costs

David's story shows the business costs of manipulation. What happened in his case is not unique. Many corporations play out this same acquisition game again and again with similar results. It's one reason corporate life can be so terrible. And it's why so many companies cannot find competent people to hire. The possibility of having to face GSRRM tactics makes it attractive to work for yourself, at a start-up, or at a smaller private business to avoid the corporate mess.

The system of manipulation in the acquiring company overtook the logical, persuasion-based system at the company that was acquired. Great people leave good jobs because of bad people (manipulators). That manipulation created competition by pushing the best people away, and they created their own rival company. By manipulating their employees, this corporation sowed the seeds of its own demise.

Manipulation drives key performance indicators in the short term at the cost of creating a toxic culture and work environment. This hits neurodivergent individuals especially hard because they have an almost allergic reaction to claims they recognize as false. (Neurotypical people, in my experience, are better at coping with lies.)

Professional relationships are crucial to maintaining a healthy business. In this case, the corporate leaders manipulated their people, and most were too afraid to say something. When trust was lost, the flow of vital information closed down. The leaders said, "The company is failing, and no one will tell me why." And their subordinates whispered, "We're going to get fired if we speak up." It's impossible to maintain trust when you're forcibly silenced and placed in groups with potential hostiles. Slowly, the entire company becomes a human resources department. The Karens overtake the entire business. That's when your profits die, and millions of dollars evaporate without a trace.

This transition from a results-first environment to constant therapy has become the norm in corporate America. You see it in schools, too. We focus on group projects instead of individual performers. The incompetent and ineffective slack off while the natural performers do all the work. The natural performers have to work twice as hard, and the slackers reap the benefits.

There are other business costs of manipulation. It makes you vulnerable to corporate espionage, reputation attacks, and extortion. When everything is based on feelings, people can leverage those feelings against you to exploit your company for whatever they want from it.

In the state where David lives, recruiting from a company you work at before you leave is illegal. So some of the upper managers at that corporation were acting illegally while getting paid for it. That's not just irreciprocal, it's legally hazardous and could ruin their reputation. That further destroys trust in the people who are still reacting to the initial manipulation.

Getting canceled is another problem. You have to pretend you believe in this week's official narrative. You fear speaking up, and it's not just about getting fired. Firing you has costs, but "canceling" you and sticking you in a corner is cheaper. If you've seen the movie *Office Space*, in which they move Milton, the unwanted employee, into the basement, take away his supplies, turn off the light, and ask him to handle their pest control problem while he works in the dark, that's one example of corporate cancellation.

All these risks come directly from manipulation in the business environment.

Relational Costs

As bad as the manipulation costs are for businesses, they're worse for families.

One of my clients was a doctor whose wife had an addiction. While he and I worked together, her alcoholism worsened. Then he found illegal prescription drugs she'd left in his car. That alone could have lost him his professional license.

I tried to help them improve their marriage. When I met her, as good as I am at detecting manipulation, I could not tell when she was lying and when she was telling the truth. She was very effective at manipulation. She often showed up obviously high or drunk but claimed she had not had anything. So I gave her sobriety tests. She failed them.

She was nice when she was sober, but she would do anything to get high. She sold my client's car behind his back. She even cashed a check of his to steal money from his business. Whenever he confronted her, she used shaming tactics by crying about how mean he was to her. My client finally drew the line. He separated from her and said he could not be with her if she couldn't stay clean.

She was lying to my client, to me, and to herself most of all. She had manipulated herself so badly, she thought she could convince herself to stop the alcohol and drugs. She also told herself she deserved to feel how the drugs made her feel.

Her thefts and lying cost him money and put his livelihood at risk. But the personal manipulations caused their marriage to fail. He truly loved her and would have done anything to help her if she'd just been honest. It was the saddest divorce I ever saw that didn't involve kids.

Think manipulation only happens in extreme examples like this? Think again. Parents manipulate their children all the time. "Do as I say, not as I do" parenting is just another way of saying "Rules for thee but not for me." That style of parenting is unfortunately mainstream. It's manipulation, and it's moralizing. "I'm your parent. The Bible says obey your parents. You have to do what I say no matter how you feel about it. No complaining."

Think about Santa Claus. Parents say, "We'll lie to you until you figure it out. But if you lie to us, we'll spank you because lying is bad."

Violence is often accompanied by manipulation. "Your child is too young to reason, so hit them to make them learn." That stunts their development and undermines your ability to communicate at their level.

Kids who end up destroying themselves by working in the adult entertainment industry often come from the most conservative religious homes. They do it to spite their parents. These parents manipulated their kids to feel shameful about themselves and about sex, and the kids want to get back at them.

Even nursing homes are a symptom of manipulation within family systems. Millions of seniors are abandoned in nursing homes. It might be true that a few have ungrateful kids. But for the vast majority, it's because the kids don't want to dig up the past trauma their parents inflicted on them through manipulation. It's easier to send them somewhere else and not let those manipulative parents inflict more potential harm in the new home.

People who were manipulated often end up manipulating their own kids, and the generational cycle of trauma continues. These echoing consequences of family dynamics repeat for generations. There's a total lack of harmony among family members. There are no intergenerational relationships, no trust, no intimacy, no heritage, and no inheritance. The grandparents may not even see the children. You may feel like you're starting from scratch with yourself and your own kids, and you have to learn to use persuasion with yourself, your spouse, your kids, your friends, and your parents.

Manipulation destroys families and destroys their future.

Public Costs

Manipulation on a national or regional scale can affect millions of people at once.

Look at China. Their Communist manipulation led to the Great Leap Forward famine and the Cultural Revolution. The US Bush administration with its WMD self-manipulation and the impeachment of Nixon (who was both manipulated and manipulating—breaking the rules to solve a problem when he didn't need to) led to a loss of trust in the US government. The Rwandan genocide manipulation drove citizens from animosity to violence, in which mothers killed other mothers in front of their children.

Political manipulation leads to corruption. That destroys trust and leaves the citizens in fear. And that fear often leads to violence—even self-inflicted. Consider the Jonestown cult. What they did was mostly legal but threatened the US power structure. They moved to South America to get away from the US government and ultimately manipulated their members to commit suicide. The manipulation leading up to the final mass murder and suicide was technically legal (or at least hard to prove illegal in court) but extremely harmful.

All this contributes to weakened communities and decreased institutional trust. And when people can't trust institutions, they faction off into their own tribal groups. That splinters the larger culture and breeds hatred, which results in irreversible damage to the moral fabric of society. The cost of public manipulation cannot be repaid.

The United Nations has not and will not be able to recover its reputation after numerous child abuse cases.[8] They used the pretense of helping the poor to give hundreds of pedophiles access to children and then covered up the abuses when they came to light. More serious than reputation is the destruction of people's lives. An organization can issue press releases and give rehearsed public

---

[8] Krista Larson and Paisley Dodds, "UN Peacekeepers in Congo Hold Record for Rape, Sex Abuse," AP News, September 23, 2017, https://apnews.com/article/united-nations-pakistan-africa-sexual-abuse-international-news-69e56ab46cab400f9f4b3753bd79c930.

apologies, but in most cases of public manipulation, it's too late to recover anything close to what was lost.

For decades, DuPont manipulated rural West Virginians and even the FDA into believing they were following health and safety regulations while pollutant chemicals poisoned people.[9] Lawsuits involving thousands of people gave affected families a path to justice. All DuPont lost was money via settlements, but the locals buried their family members. Worst of all, the financial cost to DuPont does not disincentivize them from polluting again.

Environmental Costs

Manipulation hurts our planet. The official journal of the National Academy of Sciences documented one example—how divorce greatly increases consumption of limited resources:

> Divorced households in the U.S. could have saved more than 38 million rooms, 73 billion kilowatt-hours of electricity, and 627 billion gallons of water in 2005 alone if their resource-use efficiency had been comparable to married

---

[9] Nathaniel Rich, "The Lawyer Who Became DuPont's Worst Nightmare," *The New York Times Magazine*, Januray 5, 2016, https://www.nytimes.com/2016/01/10/magazine/the-lawyer-who-became-duponts-worst-nightmare.html.

households. Furthermore, U.S. households that experienced divorce used 42–61% more resources per person than before their dissolution. Remarriage of divorced household heads increased household size and reduced resource use to levels similar to those of married households. The results suggest that mitigating the impacts of resource-inefficient lifestyles such as divorce helps to achieve global environmental sustainability and saves money for households.[10]

Fast forward to today, and we can expect the waste to be even greater. I'm not implying that married couples never experience manipulation in their relationship. I'm saying that every couple who gets divorced suffered manipulation. More marriages could be saved if couples switched to persuasion. Imagine the positive impact on the environment of win-win relationships. Marriage and family experts discuss divorce as a personal, private issue. It's not. The planet itself feels its impact.

Another notable example of manipulation's effect on the environment is the ghost city phenomenon in

---

[10] Eunice Yu and Jianguo Liu, "Environmental Impacts of Divorce," *Proceedings of the National Academy of Sciences of the United States of America* 104, no. 51 (December 2007): 20629–20634, https://doi.org/10.1073/pnas.0707267104.

China.[11] Over fifty new, planned cities sit empty and crumbling across the country. As many as 64 million empty apartments have wasted $6.8 trillion from 2009 through 2014 alone.[12] The objective was to manipulate real estate investors and developers into keeping their capital in China. They did—they tried "build it, and they will come," and no one did. At least not yet. Wade Shepard, editor-in-chief of *The China Chronicle*, writes:

> [T]he story of ghost cities in China seems to be a complex one involving economic inequality, inefficient markets, planning that may not match up with current needs, and insufficient concern about the environmental and social impact of essentially treating buildings as disposable ... [T]hese are not actually ghost cities; rather they are cities waiting for people. They may be improperly labeled when in fact they are cities whose structure is built in advance of

---

[11] Tracey Shelton, Christina Zhou, and Ning Pan, "China's Eerie Ghost Cities a 'Symptom' of the Country's Economic Troubles and Housing Bubble," June 26, 2018, ABC, https://www.abc.net.au/news/2018-06-27/china-ghost-cities-show-growth-driven-by-debt/9912186#:~:text=Built%20for%20a%20population%20that,lay%20desolate%20across%20the%20country.

[12] Jamil Anderlini, "China Has 'Wasted' $6.8tn in Investment, Warn Beijing Researchers," *Financial Times*, November 27, 2014, https://www.ft.com/content/002a1978-7629-11e4-9761-00144feabdc0.

an anticipated population movement, as in half-built Xinyang.[13]

The Economic Times further explores the waste of empty cities—most buildings in those cities and elsewhere in China have a short life.

In China, 600 new cities have been created over 65 years—the fastest pace of urbanization the world has ever seen. This has been accompanied by rapid building and rebuilding, with one estimate stating that the average building in China is demolished every 25–30 years. Frequent demolition and construction—just like John Maynard Keynes had advocated—is perceived as an economy-boosting activity. But its darker side involves forced evictions, conflicts over land and significant environmental damage.

The emergence of Chinese ghost cities is also related to a second factor: the dependence of local governments on land sales for revenue. The high value of urban land for redevelopment is leading municipal governments to reclassify and sell rural land as "urban" to developers. This creates a vicious cycle of urban expansion in which rural land is sold for urban purposes,

---

[13] Christine Ro, "Ghost Cities of China" April 30, 2015, Environment and Urbanization, https://www.environmentandurbanization.org/ghost-cities-china.

which, in turn, has urban development dependent on the reclassification of more land to replenish municipal funds. Where there is no rural land, some local authorities have even "created land"—flattening mountains and reclaiming coastal land, which come with their own economic and ecological costs.

The government together with investors have been wiping out entire biomes, replacing myriad species with . . . lifeless, unfinished concrete buildings. It's wasted wealth, wasted productivity, and wasted land. Without manipulation by the Chinese Communist Party, developers and laborers would have invested their money, time, and effort in places and industries that did something.[14]

Personal Costs

The number-one cost of manipulation on a personal level is that victims often become manipulators themselves. Because they lose trust in others, they believe their only option left is to manipulate to get their needs met. In their minds, people become objects to be controlled rather

---

[14] Vishal R. and Kala S. Sridhar, "Don't Get Haunted by Ghost Cities," *The Economic Times*, August 16, 2021, https://economictimes.indiatimes.com/blogs/urbanissues/dont-get-haunted-by-ghost-cities/.

than humans with unique value. A "do to them before they can do to me" mentality perpetuates the cycle. It's a mind virus that manipulators spread.

When people manipulate, they destroy their reputations. People say, "He's a liar." Word spreads. If caught, manipulators can find themselves ostracized by whole communities or industries.

There are also other personal costs. The chronic distrust and commitment issues make future relationships difficult. Old wounds can make it easy to be revictimized by manipulators who promise to heal the victim.

Intimacy becomes impossible without trust. A victim can find themselves totally closed off from the world around them. When that happens, what's the point of living? Manipulation can rob you of your life's purpose.

The Costs Are Too Damn High (To Ignore)

Manipulation is tempting when the short-term rewards seem so promising. Recalling the costs can help create a strong barrier against acting on those temptations. If you know that answering manipulation with manipulation attempts of your own is going to lead you down a dark path and end up destroying your ability to connect to other people, you can successfully resist the urge.

That creates an opportunity for you to use honest persuasion instead.

Now that you understand the high costs of manipulation, you see why it's so crucial to defend against it. It's not enough to stay safe. You must actively dismantle the manipulation you see happening in your environment so it doesn't destroy what is most important to you.

Next, let's talk about how you can proactively defend yourself and your environment from manipulators.

CHAPTER 4

DEFENSE AGAINST MANIPULATORS

66 **T**here is no such thing as bad publicity. All publicity is good publicity."

I agree with the above quote because of personal experience. I've gotten more bad publicity than most people can imagine. I survived cancel culture and came out stronger.

Thousands of people online accused me of being chauvinist, misogynist, a wife beater, a child abuser, a woman hater, and a white supremacist. Not a few. *Thousands*. Across both Facebook and Twitter. I blocked twenty thousand people on Facebook alone.

Three journalists at the *Florida Sun-Sentinel* newspaper picked up on the hate mob and wrote a hit piece on me. They called me a white supremacist and said I was running a seditious organization. Their article included quotes from US Congressional representatives calling me "dangerous," among other accusations.

The social media mob forced organizational clients to remove my name from contracts. One company told me privately they agreed with me but wanted to stay entirely neutral, so just my wife was publicly working with them. Then the mob of thousands tried harassing my wife, but she is not active on social media, so they just shouted into a vacuum.

This was only the beginning of the attack. Child Protective Services received two calls about me. One resulted in an investigation. I know, because a friend worked for that agency and warned me.

A public figure threatened to beat me up if he saw me. I'd had enough of the threats, so I pushed back, even offering a time and location. He didn't show up.

One member of a political extremist group threatened to get me deported and separated from my family. I suppose deportations are evil when they happen to protected groups but fantastic when they happen to your political enemies. Tolerance and coexistence, right?

The mob got hold of my phone number. Random people were sexting me faster than I could block them. My messages were a sea of pornographic photos.

You're probably wondering what I could have possibly done to earn this extreme degree of hate. Why were so many manipulators targeting me?

This nightmare took place because of two tweets I made from my primary Twitter account.

I post regularly on social media about lessons learned while coaching private clients to overcome manipulation. One observation I made is that some of the most destructive manipulators, both men and women, lack a mission in life.

Before sharing this insight on social media, I thought about just saying, "*People* without a mission." But I thought, *Why not run an A/B test? I can tweet separately about men and about women to see which gets more engagement. And the audience can tell me if it is men or women who are more interested in getting manipulation defense insights from my tweets.*

So I tweeted twice, two almost identical tweets, one about men and one about women. I got little engagement on the tweet about men. The tweet about women got 1.5 million impressions, 250,000 engagements, and nearly 17,000 comments.

Traditional conservatives who followed me understand the terminology I was using. It was their language. That was my target market around that time, the people who were engaging with me the most. I did not use the most persuasive framing of the topic. I used traditional terminology that some might consider politically incorrect, which was OK for the test I was conducting.

All tweets are market tests. How can you see what language and ideas get engagement and which don't? I wanted to see if tweets about observations from male clients or female clients get more engagement, as well as what vocabulary works best. I used several loaded terms because I wanted to maximize engagement.

But that was enough for the howling mob. They had to destroy someone for suggesting, in their minds, that women could be destructive. Journalists who found this outrage movement also attacked my organization.

What is my organization, you ask? I was cofounding a nonprofit to help Americans develop personal agency and build communities to help with home improvement projects and pitch in with bills.

Agency means getting control of yourself, not control of others. It's about improving the self-sufficiency of ordinary people. This does *not* mean "how to stop paying taxes and drink only rain water."

That organization got dragged through the mud, just like my name. All because of the manipulators who led the mob against me.

In both instances, once the tweet and the organization began getting attention, the manipulative mob came after me. They used all the classic GSRRM tactics to moralize, undermine, and shame me.

In short, they tried to destroy me. And they failed.

Lessons amid the Madness

As you might guess from the fact that you're reading my book, I survived—and thrived. I tripled my business in the following year, a direct result of the attention. The manipulation backfired.

A major reason the manipulation failed is that I was prepared to withstand manipulation. I resisted from the start and maintained my defense until the tactics got so extreme that casual observers who didn't even know me took my side.

You've probably seen the meme of the children's book cover with Adolf Hitler that says *Everyone I Don't Like Is Hitler: An Idiot's Guide to Arguing*. The manip-ulators always compare their targets to monsters like Hitler. They use false associations that convince no one. Hitler is the clue for most normal people that it's gone too far, and the manipulators are lying.

That was not the only time I faced a social media mob. Coming to the defense of people I know and respect has resulted in me and them being targeted by GSRRM. The longer an attack lasts, the worse it gets. But it always goes too far and attracts the sympathy of normal people. The manipulators sow the seeds of their own destruction.

I survived because I was prepared. You need to prepare, too.

Three Stages of Manipulation Preparation: Foundation, Defense, Allies

I not only survived the manipulators but also thrived, thanks to smart preparation. I'm going to teach you the three steps you must take in your own preparation. If you follow them, you can turn bad publicity into good publicity.

Stage 1: Build a Strong Personal Foundation

In the film *Dirty Harry*, Clint Eastwood delivers a killer line: "A man has got to know his limitations." This is key to defense in every arena, including against manipulation. You must know who you are and your personal limits.

In my case, I knew what I meant by the tweet. When people threatened to beat me in the street and take my kids away and deport me, I didn't wonder if maybe I really was a bad guy. I knew they were all lying.

One of my personal limits is to always be truthful in my public and private life. Whatever I say in private matches what I say in public. People who maintain different values in public and in private are duplicitous. When the storm hits, the clash of values breaks them.

The number-one most effective defense tactic is to always tell the truth. Tell the truth in public and in private so there is no difference. Consistency is credibility, which manipulators do not have.

Tell the truth in the simplest, most persuasive way possible. Know that you are telling the truth as you see it, and there could be variation based on other perspectives, but always know that you were honest.

It's also good to know what your interests are, what drives you, and what you care about.

I wrote those tweets and cofounded the nonprofit out of a desire to help people. I've coached women in their thirties and forties who suffered deep emotional pain because of infertility in that season of life. I would meet clients day after day, sometimes three or four daily. I was angry at society for giving them bad advice and sad for the victims. And I noticed that men who have wives and children they love are deeply motivated to change, to improve, to build. Single men without kids are difficult to motivate.

Men need duty, and women need to be loved. Both meet those needs through a spouse and children. It's almost as if our species history of sexual reproduction teaches us a lesson about happiness and life satisfaction. Parenting brings purpose and peace.

Every client I had said, "I wish my father had set me on the right course to begin with." I'd ask them, "Why don't you ask your dad about that?" Their fathers were always dead, didn't care, or were incapable of offering good advice.

I cofounded the self-sufficiency organization because I noticed clients were surrounded by manipulators at work. Worse, they needed the money or health care those jobs provided. Being manipulated at work ruined their lives, and they had no other options because they had no networks outside the office.

If you lose your job, where can you get help finding a new one? I saw a need and cofounded a group to help other people meet it.

Because I knew my driving passions, I was willing to defend them. You must also develop a willingness to defend your own interests as a form of self-protection.

I noticed in my coaching experience that men, and particularly women, were being lied to. I was often the first person who did not lie to my clients about what would make them happy. Others would tell them to climb the corporate ladder. At the end of that ladder, you only have your job. There is no family to come home to.

Big corporations have an abusive relationship with female employees. Their benefits packages often include egg freezing to give the illusion they can put family on hold to pursue their career. Egg freezing is not itself the illusion; the illusion is that women can build a successful career and still have a happy family later in life, which does not comport with human biology. Many career women wanted to start a family in their forties with frozen eggs, only to find out it was extremely difficult—if not impossible. Recent studies show the pregnancy rate of thawed eggs is as low as 1.8 percent.[15] Companies manipulate women into believing the success rate is closer to 100 percent, even if they don't explicitly state as much. "Give us the best years of your life, and we'll give you children one day."

These same companies manipulate women into taking more responsibilities and more stress with the same pay. Having so many women crying to me in private made me angry at their manipulators. I realized I had to tell the truth.

I also knew that if I toned down my tweets to be less controversial, I would get less engagement. So I used emotionally triggering words to get the point across. That was my way of spreading the message to help more people. I was willing to pay the cost of telling the truth.

When the time came, I did pay the cost. Weathering the storm spread my message to triple the audience because I was rooted in truth.

Stage 2: Build Defenses

Defenses are strong barriers you can rest behind to avoid enemy attacks. Picture a person prepared for battle. You

---

[15] "Egg-freezing: What's the Success Rate?" BBC News, February 17, 2020, https://www.bbc.com/news/health-51463488.

probably imagine a soldier in a concrete bunker or even a knight in plate mail with a sword. When medieval rulers knew they had to hold ground against attacks, they built castles.

Mental defenses against manipulation are no different. You need to build a castle and put on your armor so that manipulation attacks bounce off your defenses. Some people call this "mental frame." This is your relationship to the world and how much you will allow yourself to be moved. My frame was that someone had to tell the truth. If not me, who? If not now, when? Manipulation attempts bounced off me because I'd built my defenses knowing that attacks would come.

Don't become overconfident in your defenses. Stay humble. Anyone can be manipulated. Castles fall, suits of armor have weak spots, and a Kevlar vest is no match for a nuke. Shame over being manipulated makes future manipulation easier. Accept that some people will try to manipulate you. When you fall for manipulation, don't be ashamed. Learn from that gap in your defense and fix the weakness.

Another way to stay safe is to trust but verify. Build defensive measures into your information networks. Set boundaries and triggers you control with premade action plans.

Cultivate a willingness to be disagreeable. To be insulted. To be called "not nice." Manipulators will call you a number of horrible names to crack your defenses.

When you recognize their tactics, you remove their ability to hurt you.

For example, I never respond to insults. If you insult me, you get blocked. I always avoid answering insincere questions. If hostile? Ignore. If not hostile but curious? Make them do the work. It's jujitsu. Hold on until they get tired. It's easier to deflect a punch than to throw one. Let manipulators expend their energy. Respond when they are exhausted.

Just like with castle walls, laying siege takes a toll on the attackers. They get more cartoonish, even goofy, as subtle manipulation stops working. They reach the point at which the insanity is unbelievable, even to strangers who don't know you. That's when the Hitler comparisons come out. They hang themselves with their own rope.

What about silence? Does silence mean consent and an admission of guilt? Sometimes. You can remain silent and let the insanity speak for itself, unless you've got a killer reply that deflates enemy momentum. In that case, insults help you.

I am strong, tall, and in shape. If someone accuses me of being a skinny geek no woman wants, all I have to do is post a photo of my physique and/or my three children—not showing their faces, of course. The accuser loses all credibility.

Remember that manipulation has three parties: you, the manipulator, and the audience. Manipulators are trying to break you down in front of the audience. But their tactics are disgusting, and if the those watching ever recognizes what the exploiter is really doing, they will turn on them.

Nobody likes a puppet master. Everybody hates having their strings pulled. They can easily imagine being used. So you can simply persuade the audience by telling the truth. Let your behavior contrast with the manipulator's, and their smear job becomes obvious.

You don't even have to win to earn respect. The film *Cool Hand Luke* is a great example. The manipulators kill him in the end, but the audience respects the protagonist for holding his principles. The more disrespectful the deceivers, the more your audience will respect you. Remember what is important to you. I am not interested in a public conversation with people who do not care about truth. I don't want people who consent to being manipulated reading my work or following me online. People respect me for drawing that line.

Take steps to get your voice heard when appropriate. In business, you want decision makers to know the truth before they hear lies from manipulators. The first story people hear is the one they'll believe. Letting people hear the lie first poisons the well. State the truth loudly and clearly so any lie is obvious. As you plan, make prevention of poisoning the well your number one priority.

Another way to prevent manipulation is to prevent yourself from being a target. Keanu Reeves goes to great lengths to prevent himself from being in a compromising situation, so no one would ever believe any accusation. Contrast this with President Joe Biden, who has been photographed doing what looks like fondling underage children. He's a target for accusations because he already looks guilty.

Don't look guilty. Curate your presence and appearance to project honesty. That means be authentic *and* look authentic. Dishonest curation is fragile. If people find dishonesty in one area, the house of cards collapses.

Corporations provide a great example of dishonest curation. They announce, "We gave millions to charities last year." The part they whisper in private is "We gave millions to charities last year to signal our virtue while lowering our tax liabilities." They also tell employees, "We're a family." Yet they approve massive layoffs. Saying "We're a dysfunctional family who use each other" would have been more honest. What else are they lying about?

Once you've built your personal defenses, search for weak spots in them. Eliminate personal triggers you don't control, which are like chinks in the armor. If people are calling you fat, and you are, and that bothers you, that's a personal trigger. Take steps to get in shape so that the trigger won't work.

You cannot shame a man who has nothing to be ashamed of. If you've always told the truth, you won't be ashamed of lies told about who you are, so you probably don't have chinks in your armor. Most shame is uncovering something you've been dishonest about.

In my case, I removed my name from several business contracts so that my partners would not be harmed if the cancel mob came for me with false accusations. That was a chink in my armor that enemies tried to use against me. Now they can't.

Avoid fights you can't win. Do you suspect someone in your life has an issue like borderline personality disorder or narcissistic personality disorder that makes rational discussion impossible? Consult a professional, then cut ties if possible. Block abusive users online. Remove potential fights before they happen.

Enforce reciprocity. If people come to me with sincere, honest questions, I give sincere, honest answers. If they attack me, I push back, block them online, and immediately address any weaknesses they uncover. That removes their ability to attack. "Blocking" abusive people from your life works, too.

Defenses are key to stopping problems before they can hurt you.

Stage 3: Recruit Allies

Castles are worthless without troops. You need people you can trust to come to your aid.

Surround yourself with people who will be honest with you no matter what. Tell the truth, and you'll be surrounded by people who want the truth. Without effective lies, they cannot manipulate; they must persuade. You want people in your corner, friend group, and network who are persuaders, not manipulators. This means you'll have a smaller but more reliable social network, which matters for what's next.

Manipulation is social warfare. You need people who will help with your defense. In my case, those friends were people who defended me in the comments. They waded in and presented counterarguments so the audience could find the truth among the lies. I recruited ten friends to report people who posted death threats or used words offensive to protected classes. Those accounts were banned, removing their ability to attack.

At the corporate level, you need employees who are sheepdogs to find manipulators. Most people do not have the personality to protect themselves or others from manipulators. You must be proactive in removing threats from the environment. That also means teaching your people how to become immune to manipulation.

One key is to make sure your allies understand the dangers of manipulation. Some of my friends who had come to my defense got triggered and began reciprocating with manipulative tactics, like shaming. They were going too far, so I sent out a short video explaining how to become immune to manipulation. That made our mutual defense stronger.

If people defending you are manipulated, that's worse than no one defending you. Numbers are not important in social warfare. Behavior is. I blocked twenty thousand people and had ten friends on my side. I even gave them admin rights to my business profile. Those angry mobs got no value from the experience. I did, and I won.

We didn't try to fight all the battles. We picked the craziest comments and accusations to respond to. For example, the size of my genitals came up often, so I reframed the insults as compliments. "All these women are talking about my genitals." Shame had no power over me.

The flip side of this approach is to avoid people who will undermine or manipulate your defenses. Some people on your side are not honest. They are willing to use manipulation as their primary strategy. When they come to your defense with those tactics, you look like the bad guy.

Curate who sends messages on behalf of your organization so they are coherent and truthful. I've been a part of an organization in which a spouse was manipulating an individual in leadership to spread specific messages. We had to remove that person from the team.

Anyone who would use manipulation cannot be in your life. Fill your circle with people who will reject all GSRRM tactics no matter what. You must know they will take your side against the mob.

On old battleships, crew members could mutiny, but it wouldn't work if the officers held firm. As long as your castle holds, you're safe. The biggest threats are the people inside who would open the doors to the enemy. Make sure you curate your allies.

From Preparation to Victory

Take all three of these steps before you do anything that might be considered controversial publicly, on social media, or in your organization. You have to expect manipulation, know how and from whom it will come, even which tactics will be used. That way, you can stay one step ahead and avoid emotional triggers. Once you're prepared, lead the situation instead of reacting. Follow those steps, and you can win like I did.

You might wonder if fighting fire with fire is ever justified. Can persuasion alone defeat extreme manipulation? My perspectives on these important topics are more nuanced than you may have heard before. Let's address them next.

CHAPTER 5

PERSUASION VERSUS MANIPULATION

If you think smart, beautiful people are immune to manipulation, you're wrong.

I coached a woman who endured twenty-one years of manipulation from her husband. The first time we met, I thought, *Oh my goodness, she's gorgeous*. She said she was forty-seven years old, but I'd have thought she was twenty-seven.

She was an Eastern European immigrant living in the UK with her manipulative British husband. She realized after twenty-one years of marriage that she was nothing more than a trophy wife to him, and he'd pushed her back and forth the entire time to keep her unstable. "I would love you more if you just did this one thing for me. Oh, you did? But you didn't act like you liked it.

Why do you hate me? Show me you love me." The wife couldn't keep pretending she was happy to try to please him anymore (would could?), so he demanded a divorce.

In truth, the husband did not know how to respond to his wife's sweetness, honesty and feminine vulnerability. She fell for him because at the start he was kind, loving, and romantic. After they got married, he undermined her sense of self while pushing her into acting against her wishes. When she reacted, he withdrew attention or lashed out at her. He made her believe she was the problem for not giving him everything he wanted, even when what he wanted was unclear or unreasonable.

My client spent half our early sessions wondering what she did wrong. Recounting the emotional abuse left her in tatters, so we had to end our sessions early.

What could bring such a stunning woman to allow herself to be abused like this? When I asked, I learned she'd been manipulated by her parents. It took two years of coaching for her to extricate herself from the trauma left by upbringing. Manipulation can be healed, but not without help.

Manipulation in the family usually gets no blow-back. People will drop hints, but society forbids your friends and loved ones from saying, "That person is manipulating you."

People don't speak up because they're afraid you'll hate them for it. Or that the manipulator will come after them next. Those fears may be justified, since built-in plausible deniability makes manipulation legal. Now, what is built-in plausible deniability, and how does it make manipulation legal? An example may be a parent scolding a child and calling him "good for nothing." When challenged on this verbal abuse by another parent, the manipulative parent simply says, "I'm his parent. It's for his own good. Besides, that's how my parents talked to me, and I turned out OK." Sadly, this coercion is legal because no law governs how parents discipline their children. Unlike victims of physical abuse, manipulators' targets have no laws or resources to protect them. Manipulation is difficult to escape when the very person who should be protecting you is your enemy.

Why do manipulators choose to hurt honest people? Because they're trying to get the best outcome they can, even if it hurts others. In my client's case, marrying someone out of his league made her husband look and feel good. He was selfish, and she was high in conscientiousness, the type of person to do what was right even if it was painful. Manipulation made him feel secure in their relationship because it made him feel powerful, in control. Without manipulation, he feared that he couldn't keep her, so when he did, he felt accomplished.

Corporations manipulate employees in similar ways. Manipulative bosses fear workers will slack off and steal if given an inch of trust. These managers cannot trust because they are not trustworthy. They project their behavior onto others.

What could my client's husband have done differently? He could have connected with her on an honest level and shared what he wanted without coercing her into performing tricks like a dog. She needed a proper emotional connection with mutual trust. So did he. That's persuasion.

Persuasion Is Win-Win; Manipulation Is Win-Lose

Earlier in this book, we introduced the difference between persuasion and manipulation. You've learned to defend yourself from the dangers of manipulation. It's time to teach you about persuasion.

Manipulation means treating people like objects. They're obstacles to be removed in the pursuit of goals. Persuasion is when you treat people like people. You need to work with them to accomplish your goals, which means helping them meet their goals so they have an incentive to help you.

Note that both cases involve moving people. You can move people ethically or unethically. It comes down to how honestly you engage with them about what you want and how you leave them when you've accomplished what you wanted.

When you openly share and offer to exchange needs and when you fulfill others' needs so they're better off than when you started working together, that's persuasion. Everything is on the table, and you both benefit together instead of one side exploiting the other for personal gain.

Persuasion applies outside relationships, too. For example, persuasion is when a dating coach says, "I will teach you how to understand women and build healthy relationships." Manipulation is when a pickup artist guru says, "I will teach you seven ways to trick women into bed with you, and you won't believe number six. But if none of them work, women are broken, and it's your fault, loser."

Some fitness product companies market their goods with messaging like "Healthy at any size," accompanied by pictures of morbidly obese individuals using those products. The company's marketing leaders don't want to risk losing customers by telling them the truth—obesity causes chronic disease and, in most cases, an early death. The persuasive alternative would be "You can become healthy starting at any size." The company could feature fitness journeys of unhealthy people who, using their products, transformed their bodies, improving self-confidence and overall happiness.

If it's hard to picture companies using persuasive marketing strategies instead of manipulating customers, it's because we're conditioned to accept manipulation as normal.

Individuals and corporations aren't the only manipulators. Governments also manipulate their own citizens. They often follow up their propaganda by applying force to coerce their people's submission. China's Tiananmen Square Massacre and the forced layoffs in US Federal Services in response to President Biden's vaccine mandate are clear examples of manipulation, propaganda, and use of force against dissenters.

At this point you might ask, "Is it ever moral to use manipulation tactics?" In reality, manipulation doesn't make you a bad person so much as it makes you inauthentic. So the question becomes "When is it OK to be inauthentic?"

I approach this topic the same way I approach the question "When is it OK to harm someone?" The answer is when self-defense demands it.

The book *The Gift of Fear* by Gavin de Becker details stories of women who escaped from serial killers by manipulating them. It teaches women how to leverage manipulation on their attackers in order to get away. When a serial killer is trying to murder you, manipulation tactics in the moment can save your life.

That really is the line. Justification for harming someone else requires clear and present danger without other options. If you've got the time and ability to use persuasion, you should. Otherwise you're choosing to manipulate out of convenience or comfort, which is irreciprocal and immoral.

How to Resist the Temptation to Manipulate

It often seems easier to move someone by force than to take the time to explain. How do you resist the temptation? The answer is learning to prioritize authenticity and openness over convenience. Using persuasion instead will pay dividends in the long run. You won't expose yourself to consequences or have to unravel the tangled knots you've tied your relationships into. Spend a little time now to avoid a big disaster later.

You also need to unlearn the wrong lessons you've been carrying around. If you believe that persuasion leaves you vulnerable and that vulnerability is bad, the barrier to persuasion might seem too high for you to climb. You may feel like manipulation is your only option. That's why serial manipulators keep coercing others even as their consequences pile up. They don't believe there's any other way.

To stop manipulating, my client's husband would have had to start trusting people. But first, he would have needed to trust himself. Which he didn't, because he did not trust his parents.

If your parents aren't reliable, you cannot see anyone else as reliable. Even after twenty-one years of being married to a sweet woman who worked hard to nurture him, my client's husband couldn't bring himself to say,

"I can trust my wife." The healing can't begin from outside. It has to be a personal choice first.

I start every personal relationship by offering trust, and I know that can leave me vulnerable to betrayal. But I know that if I get hurt extending trust to the right person, I am resilient enough to endure the consequences. My client's husband didn't share that faith in himself. His betrayal by a previous wife had left him determined not to trust another woman again.

I see that problem a lot in second marriages. When both parties lack trust, the relationship ends quickly. But my client believed she needed to do the right thing even at a high cost to herself—so she perceived everything that went wrong as her fault.

The Vulnerability Secret

"People can be trusted. And I can trust people." To replace manipulation with persuasion in our relationships, we need to believe both.

Does trust leave you open to bad actors? Absolutely. What's the alternative—a life of suspicion, loneliness, and misery with people who resent you for manipulating them? No, thanks. I'll take the occasional pain. And I'll build enough boundaries that bad actors will get caught on the outermost fence before they can do much harm.

That's the way to live—not huddling in your bunker, terrified to accept love.

Admit vulnerability. A wolf will show its neck or belly to build trust in the pack. Modern armies cut soldiers' hair short so the enemy can't grab them from behind when they retreat. In contrast, history's greatest warriors had long hair to show they wouldn't turn tail and run away. They openly displayed vulnerability to show their strength and courage.

Men like my client's husband need to open up emotionally, allowing others to get close to them. They should show they are strong enough to shoulder the risk of opening up.

Showing vulnerability to trustworthy people requires you to be strong. Showing vulnerability is like kryptonite to untrustworthy people. It's a test. Your intentional display of vulnerability reveals who the other person really is. For example, before I accept a new client, I want to vet them. I admit I'm busy and that I don't have time in my schedule for clients who will not do the work. So I ask them if they'll do the work. If they answer with absolutes and speak with extreme self-confidence, that's a tell for self-manipulation, meaning I likely cannot trust them. I expressed a need—to work with reliable people with my limited schedule—and that is vulnerability. The vulnerability is brief and intentional, not sustained or accidental.

The old show *Gunsmoke* is another example of selective vulnerability. Sheriff Matt Dillon, the main character, killed dozens of people without coming off as a mass murderer. Whenever a troublemaker waved a gun around, instead of pulling his own gun, Dillon would rest his hands by his belt buckle as if to say, "I'm not afraid of you. I'll let you initiate this fight and still kick your butt."

Matt Dillon showed strength by intentionally selecting when to show vulnerability. And the other characters trusted him. Even his enemies trusted that taking a swing at him wouldn't work.

When you're brutally honest and vulnerable, you're giving people a choice. You're also making your behavior predictable. That establishes trust, even with enemies.

Persuasion builds bridges. Trusting you allows your enemy to open dialogue instead of jumping to violence. Through honest conversation and persuasion, you can come to an agreement with most people who would otherwise have stayed your enemies.

This is why openness is so important at the beginning of any relationship, whether a first date or a job interview. Honesty is partial vulnerability. You may not get what you want, but you're willing to be open about your expectations and desires. That allows others to trust you, even if they're not friendly yet.

I often get asked, "Should I do business with friends?"

Men I call friends are men I would trust with my life. Therefore, I only do business with friends. If I can't trust you with my money, then I can't trust you, so you can't be my friend. Better to find out you are untrustworthy and lose a few dollars than to find out and lose my life.

Opportunities to Persuade Ethically

See your wants as opportunities, not as threats you need to mitigate. An unmet need is a chance to be more honest about that need. It's also a chance to see how other people respond when you share total openness. If they run from vulnerability or attempt to overcome your boundaries, you dodged a bullet. If they share their needs in return and seek a way to satisfy both sides, you're in business. That's true in financial dealings and in marriage.

My client's husband saw her as a social-sexual object—a means to an end. He had no concern for her needs.

We all have objects in our lives. They submit to our will. In war, the enemy is an object in the way of your survival.

But that paradigm doesn't work in intimate relationships. Successful marriages can't be war. Neither can parent-child relationships.

In the absence of cooperation, manipulators have to "break" the object. Public school teachers often act this way toward little boys. My son was resisting his teacher's authority in the classroom when she tried to act on him like an object—a student who must be made to obey instructions, even unclear, unnecessary instructions, without question. My wife had to tell her to ask for our son's help instead of ordering him around.

Breaking spouses, children, and employees like horses harms them. If you care about their needs, you won't do it.

Doing harm comes with a cost. Your kids will become susceptible to manipulation—and will use it right back at you. Lies make it easy to escape manipulation, so they become liars.

Yes, it's harder to reason with children than to command them. But no sensible person wants to live in a system where might makes right. People living under tyranny eventually rebel against it.

Some parenting manipulation is outright emotional abuse. Spanking is not only about physical pain; it's also about humiliation and fear of impending humiliation. That's manipulation. If you carry that approach over to every interaction, your child will learn you're out to coerce them into behaviors. That violates healthy familial trust.

The cooperative, persuasive approach takes more energy but creates better outcomes. You offer people enough value to change their preferences, which improves their view of you. Your preferences may also need to change, but that's OK because preferences are malleable.

What could my client's husband have done? He could have helped his wife work through her childhood trauma. He could have ensured he built up her sense of security in their relationship. When she came to him with complicated emotions, he needed to be solid. Instead, he called her "needy."

Her unmet needs were opportunities for building bonds of trust. Meeting her needs would have made her willing to meet his needs, including in the bedroom. Instead, he undermined her because he didn't trust her.

Let's take another look at the cooperative, persuasive approach to parenting. We'll use brushing your teeth as an example. Overt manipulation would be holding your kids down and brushing their teeth for them. Coercive manipulation would be shame. "You get a sticker" quickly becomes "You don't get a sticker, and look how many you've missed this week."

Persuasive parenting means working with the child to provide age-appropriate videos and books explaining the benefits of toothbrushing. This way can also be fun. My twins get a song and playtime. They associate toothbrushing with soothing activities and positive outcomes. If they had constant access to toothbrushes, they'd brush their teeth all day.

The cooperative, persuasive approach also works in business. LEGO Group is an example of healthy products and persuasion. They will only hire people who are already Adult Fans Of LEGO (AFOL). And they treat people like family. Need to attend your kid's birthday? Pregnant? Injured? Take plenty of time off. LEGO only fires people for truly terrible behavior. They have fifth-generation employees. I've met hundreds of LEGO employees, and every one of them loved the company.

Why Persuasion Beats Manipulation in the Long Run

Is manipulating someone to do the right thing moral? Only if the intended act and circumstances are moral.

There's no virtue in losing weight if I point a gun at your head and say, "Start eating right, or I'm going to shoot you." You didn't become a responsible adult; you acted under duress. My manipulation seemed to have a good motive, but it harmed you and didn't achieve a sustainable good outcome.

Consider the successful entrepreneurs and entertainers who get asked, "What's your secret?" Often, they lie. "I worked hard and got lucky. You can be anything you want." That may be true, but it deceives the public into believing work ethic and good fortune are enough. They're not. The unintended consequence is the mass disillusionment of millions of failed entrepreneurs and entertainers, many of whom succumb to addiction and suicide. If they were honest, the public figures would say, "I have a high IQ, I came from a supportive family who gave me funding to get started, and then I worked hard and got lucky. Not everyone can be anything they want."

Lying for your own benefit, even to save face, produces low return on investment (ROI). Yet reciprocity for mutual gain yields the highest ROI. You can almost always persuade the other party to accept such a situation. But you have to take a breath and apply the time and effort. When you do that, your outcomes improve.

Manipulation requires constant reinforcement. Persuasion is self-reinforcing because both sides want to sustain the relationship. So put in the time and effort to create a cycle of perpetual good. You'll be glad you did.

CHAPTER 6

A WORLD WITHOUT MANIPULATION

At this point, you understand how manipulation robs you of the best parts of life. You're ready to build a life totally free from manipulation. But you have one problem. You've never seen such a life. How can you emulate something you've never seen?

Let's take this chapter to explore what your life and the world at large can—and will—look like once you clean out the manipulators and start implementing healthy persuasion in every relationship.

Your World without Manipulation

When you're immune to manipulation, no one can move you against your will. People have to persuade you or get out of your life.

That means you don't manipulate others either—you have to persuade. You must consider how to give value. Becoming a net value creator changes everything. No more fear of job loss. No fear of divorce. You become too valuable for anyone to get rid of. That means they'll work harder to keep you and provide more value in return. You'll get back more than you give away.

Through persuasion, you'll get along with people better and get to know them faster because you'll foster more trust. You may have fewer relationships over-all, but the remaining relationships will be high trust, lower maintenance, and low frustration. Five close friends are worth more than fifty acquaintances trying to manipulate you.

Embracing persuasion also brings lower anxiety. You'll be able to relax because you'll have a passive manipulation detector running in the background keeping you safe.

In short, you'll be more stable, and so will your relationships.

Once you stop manipulating yourself, you can trust your own judgment. You make the right decision rapidly without second-guessing. And if a decision doesn't work out, you let it go because you know you made the best decision possible with the information you had at the time. No self-doubt or blame.

From fitness and finances to career and long-term relationships, you won't wait for others to tell you what to do. You'll accept personal responsibility in all areas of your life because you'll no longer be manipulating yourself into believing it's all someone else's fault. And you won't be solely responsible for maintaining your relationships because both sides will be providing value to each other. Every relationship will be a team effort. With persuasion, you can relax into love.

That was the big picture. What does a manipulation-free life look like in detail?

Manipulation-free marriages build emotional intimacy. Each spouse can be honest without fearing the other will exploit secrets. Once you share your wants and needs, you've taught the other person how to hurt you. It's not a lack of communication skills that hinders most marriages; it's the fear of vulnerability from sharing needs and wants.

A new mom who wants to stay home with the baby may fear her husband will use his position as breadwinner to manipulate her. How could anyone maintain a marriage like that? Manipulation and even the fear of manipulation can drive a couple toward divorce.

Manipulation even makes it hard to share sexual needs. Knowing the other partner has what you can't get anywhere else creates fear of being controlled. Sex—and money—become bargaining chips in most long-term romantic relationships. Sometimes this toxicity is an unintentional childhood habit.

Children who have to "be good" to get rewards learn not to trust those they're most emotionally intimate with—their parents. A parent who manipulates a child breaks trust early in life and destroys the capacity to persuade in the teenage years and beyond.

Compelling a virtue is not virtuous. Manipulating your spouse into giving you sex or money is unethical. If you are manipulating, you are not offering value.

What does living without manipulation look like? I'll show you with details from my own life.

Early on, my wife and I had conversations about how to build a marriage that consisted of more than obligatory exchanges. We needed to offer emotional, mental, and spiritual value to each other. And we knew that manipulation would ruin us. So we agreed never to manipulate each other about household chores, childcare, budgeting and finances, spending, or even sexual intimacy. Otherwise, we might end up in a standoff because of a lack of trust.

Manipulation versus persuasion makes the difference between a transactional marriage and a reciprocal marriage. Reciprocity does not mean tracking who did what for whom, like a business agreement. In a transaction, you police the other person to make sure you're paid what you think you're owed. In contrast, reciprocity means policing yourself to avoid taking more than you give.

Transactionality is exactly why "choreplay" doesn't work. The woman wants the chore done, so she pays her man with attention. Or the man doesn't want to level up his career, so he offers to do exactly 50 percent of the chores if she gets a job outside the home. Is it possible to work fifty/fifty and do chores fifty/fifty? And to maintain that balance with clear communication that prevents resentment? Only with persuasion. But few couples discuss these arrangements with full honesty.

I've built a manipulation-free career. The men's group I run has outlawed manipulation. We persuade each other by giving encouragement, which adds value and helps us grow stronger. Love is motivation. We don't enact shame. Externally imposed shame is ineffective, unproductive, and unethical. We do build boundaries with expectations. When a man crosses a line, he's told what he did was wrong and is asked to make it right so everyone benefits.

My goal in the men's group—and in all professional relationships—is to choose persuasion over manipulation. Using persuasion to get the new client, promotion, or job means knowing you are adding value. My instinct is to add more value than I promised. Underpromising and overdelivering are powerful persuasion, particularly in long-term relationships.

Collaborating on projects in a manipulation-free career protects you from manipulating yourself into relationships that do not help you. The same goes for staying away from manipulative people.

Beware niceness. It's inherently dishonest but deceptively friendly manipulation that fails the reciprocity test. That's why excessive niceness can give the sense that something's just not right. Niceness should not be confused with kindness. The former is a superficial manipulation tactic. The latter comes from genuine love and willingness to give without expecting anything in return.

The question is how to spot the signs of niceness. "Love bombs" and feel-good promises that bait you into hazards against your better judgment are examples of such signs. (Love bombing is an attempt to manipulate a person by excessive demonstrations of attention and false affection. The target is overwhelmed by the emotion and is often shamed into reciprocating with actions that primarily benefit the manipulator.)

Many people have terrible family lives. Manipulative business leaders realize that and promise a replacement family without delivering on the implied guarantees. It would be honest to say, "We're like a family—a dysfunctional family." But they don't tell the truth.

Meanwhile, if you work at a company that tells the truth, you know where you stand at all times. "We're not a family. Every year, we fire the bottom 10 percent of performers." Leadership is not "nice," but they are authentic, and it's obvious how to keep your job.

Similarly, companies that call their workers "family" and treat them like it with flexible hours and industry-leading benefits are practicing reciprocity. Often, multiple generations have worked for the company, and the company rewards that loyalty decade after decade.

Now, how do you tell the difference between honest companies and "nice" but manipulative ones? Usually, reciprocal organizations are open to blunt internal feedback. Truth comes before face in a high-trust environment. Both mercenary and family-style companies generally foster openness and transparency. They're governed by the rule of law, so everyone knows where they stand, but the rule of law isn't the basis for their behavior. Respect is what guides them. When they act upon individual members in their network, they act with respect for the dignity of that individual beyond what the law requires. That is persuasion.

The World without Manipulation

In a world without manipulation, there are no massive propaganda pushes that benefit the elite class at everyone else's expense. Once liberated from manipulation, people will find irreciprocal arrangements unacceptable and intolerable, thus outlawing such behavior at all levels of society and in all areas of public life.

I'm not saying every human being will be perfect. There will be no end to people who want to be manipulators. But those would-be manipulative employers, politicians, and family members will have little chance to succeed. Zero-tolerance policies toward any manipulative tactics, no matter how small, would be better for us all.

Does this mean we must all protect ourselves from manipulation? Yes, for a start. The people who are strong enough to protect themselves must learn how. From there, we offer everyone in society protection from manipulation. Every form of manipulation, from a politician's promise to a corporation's quality guarantee, ought to be legally binding and enforceable by law. Until then, we the people must punish manipulators.

My friend, ghostwriter Joshua Lisec, pointed out that journalists, politicians, and institutional experts who use superfluous adverbs are not telling the truth. For example, they say, "*credibly* accused" to mean "we need you to believe this accuser" or "the president *literally* said" to mean "the president did not use these literal words, but we want you to think he did."

Joshua has been effective at changing perceptions of leaders. Manipulation through the written word is now easy to spot. The meme is spreading. Even if people who practice Joshua's adverb rule don't know the truth, they can spot when something is wrong. Excessive use of adverbs discredits a public figure as a manipulator not to be trusted, or even listened to.

The adverb example is neither enforceable nor prosecutable. Nobody gets into any official trouble for splattering adverbs across their writing. Still, adverb spotting is a decentralized, distributed tactic to identify lying manipulators and protect as many people as possible.

Can we get rid of these liars? No. Those journalists are not going anywhere. But when we shift away from manipulation, their lies won't be effective. When we withdraw our consent to hearing lies, they lose the incentive to tell lies. They'll have to report the truth. That will be a shock!

Remove the adverbs, and the lie is obvious. When "the president *essentially* said" becomes "the president said," and people can go and read the president's actual words, the liar's reputation is destroyed forever. Consider the Covington kid—Nick Sandmann—who the media lied about but later received a settlement from several companies over those lies. We can leverage truth against the lies and win.

A world without manipulation is within our grasp. We just need to find the courage to demand it.

Imagine . . .

Imagine an economy built on companies demonstrating value to sell rather than using emotional manipulation. You may only now come to the realization that most consumer goods, from packaged food to grooming products, are sold via manipulation. Secret shame and people's programmed ability to manipulate themselves define our economy. Imagine if it was built on honesty instead.

What if politicians, leaders, and public authorities were forced to deploy persuasion instead of manipulation? They would not be able to turn groups against each other, which they do by telling different stories to different groups. With no more playground gossip to foment strife for fun and profit, everything the left and the right hate about government would decrease in severity. Artificial problems both parties use to enrich themselves and their backers would disappear.

The problem with identity politics isn't identity itself—it's the artificial manipulation used to divide groups along religious, racial, and other identity traits. Honest leaders should resolve conflicts between groups through win-win persuasion. This may not be a quick process, but it is effective and brings long-lasting benefits. Where manipulation masks over problems or creates new problems, persuasion prevents future issues. Abandoning manipulation and using persuasion can bring peace to everyone involved.

First and foremost, in a world without manipulation, we'd be able to trust strangers again. That would boost our ability to form a functioning society based on healthy networks and relationships. Our whole culture would heal.

Isn't that a world you want to live in? You can. The first step is to reject all manipulation and embrace persuasion instead.

CHAPTER 7

FREQUENTLY ASKED QUESTIONS ABOUT MANIPULATION (AND THEIR ANSWERS)

T his section covers tactics, topics, and takeaways that often come up in client conversations. Feel free to study all these special cases as most people will face most of them at some point in their lives. Refer back for a quick antimanipulation refresher as needed.

FAQs about Family and Personal Manipulation

We'll start with common difficult situations in our personal lives.

How Do I Respond to a Manipulative Partner?

Stop accepting the manipulation by setting and communicating clear boundaries with your partner while reassuring them that you still love them. This can be scary at first. You fear losing someone you are attracted to and perhaps intimately bonded with. However, if being honest destroys a relationship, it was already too late to save it.

Setting boundaries is changing the rules of the relationship, a rejection of behavior that was accepted in the past. You need to be clear that your partner is not being rejected, only the manipulative behavior.

Don't expect your partner to be immediately thrilled to learn that they can no longer use manipulation to get their needs met. Show them how they can persuade you. Let them know that they can still get what they need.

One of my young female clients joined a Zoom call with friends from school. Some of those friends were male. Her boyfriend found out she was talking to some guys, and he dumped her, claiming that she was "cheating" (shaming).

This young woman was crushed. She couldn't understand what she'd done wrong, but she was desperate to fix it and get her boyfriend back. She's smart but very high in agreeableness, so the manipulation shook her to the core. As of this writing, I'm working with her and her mother to help them understand the manipulation.

Young men are told to manipulate women through a push-pull tactic of offering and then withdrawing attention. Many wounded partners come to me for help figuring out what they're doing wrong to be treated poorly. When I make these clients aware of the manipulation, they can't believe it at first.

That young woman's vulnerability to manipulation came from observing her parents' relationship. It took me five sessions to help the mother see that her husband had been manipulating her for over twenty years. Manipulation had become normalized in that family.

It takes a delicate touch and a lot of patience to help someone realize their partner is manipulating them. I can't bluntly say, "You've been manipulated into thinking this person loves you."

Mark 8:22–26 tells how Jesus Christ healed a blind man. First he restored a little of the man's eyesight and asked, "What do you see?" And the man said, "I can see people. They look like trees, but they are walking around." It took three tries to give that blind man all his eyesight back. Could Jesus have done it in one try? Sure. But he chose to ease the man into sight so he wouldn't be overwhelmed.

In the same way, it's disorienting to suddenly go from living under manipulation to seeing the truth. Many people must be gently and slowly brought into the light.

Imagine you know that your friend's wife is cheating on him, but he doesn't want to believe it. You can ask questions to make him think about the answers, but you can't shake him and scream, "Your wife is cheating on you!" He'll direct his fear at you in the form of anger.

Your first step is to stop denying the manipulation's existence. If you can take that first step, everything else will follow.

How Do I Deal with Manipulative Parents?

I worked with one set of clients who couldn't stop manipulating each other. The wife married the husband to get away from her controlling parents, yet she kept taking their advice. They ran her marriage into the ground because they enjoyed the drama. Her parents even played the family's sons-in-law against each other. If one of them couldn't live up to the parents' arbitrary standards, they tried to shame him into it. That manipulation caused animosity through the whole family.

The parents were white collar, and the client's husband was blue collar. If he wanted to grow a mustache, ride a motorcycle, or work out, they'd complain. Instead of helping him develop his natural talents, they tried to force him into their box.

Almost all in-law problems follow that pattern. They want you to be more like they think they are. The way to gain their respect is to boldly resist their attempts to mold you. Manipulators will come to see you as a real person, not an object. Or they'll reject and avoid you. Either way, you become free.

How Can I Shield My Kids from Manipulative Grandparents?

Don't let your children's grandparents—either your parents or your spouse's—lie in front of your children. When children interact with manipulative grandparents, one parent should always be present to know what's being said. Correct messages as necessary, even if doing so causes friction. Your whole family should defend your kids from lying.

Lying is not the extent of grandparent manipulation. The reality is that grandparents often feel detached from outcomes with grandkids because they're not the ones responsible for the children's upbringing, so they might take a more cavalier response to shaping behaviors.

Shaming, rewarding, moralizing, and other practices may wound your child in unexpected ways if their grandparents spout off about some perceived issue in the child's behavior. These harsh criticisms or forced expectations may lead your child down dark paths if they stop feeling safe with their family.

Bear in mind that the problems you experienced growing up are unlikely to have disappeared overnight. That doesn't give you free license to attack your parents for every perceived fault, but you do need to make sure their approach to your children matches your own. Having a sit-down discussion with them about your goals for your children and laying out clear expectations can get you all on the same page. If they reject this approach, that tells you they're unsupportive of your parenting. That's a red flag that they may undercut you with the children when you're not around.

And there are always genuine problems you might need to address. Personality disorders, attachment problems, and addictions are serious concerns that need to be fully addressed before you trust your children alone with their grandparents. And some of them might make it impossible to allow your children to ever be alone with them. Sharing blood does not give someone carte blanche to treat your children however they choose. The family should share a united goal of raising healthy children who can achieve the best outcomes in their lives. If serious problems cause your parents to act with hostility toward those plans, you need to take a serious look at what is best for your children's mental and emotional safety.

How Do I Handle In-law Problems?

Spouses must have a stronger bond between each other than with their parents or their kids. As the Bible says, you should become "one flesh." Making the parent relationship secondary makes it difficult to pry spouses apart.

Maintain open communication in your marriage. Spouses should tell each other if parents, in-laws, or friends deride them. Don't let those secrets fester. Air them out and handle them right away. The backbiters will complain because they want to gain leverage over the two of you. Push back with complete openness. When everyone knows you don't keep secrets, they stop trying to play you against each other.

The same goes for people who give direct insults. I once heard a client say, "My in-laws told my wife they could not manage her, so she was broken." If his wife hadn't told him that, she would have been stuck with that message inside her head. Because she shared it aloud to her husband, he was able to help counteract the messaging.

Attachment specialist Adam Lane Smith often says, "Spouses need strong, healthy attachment to each other. And that requires transparency." Total transparency is the key to a healthy marriage because it forces you to deal with problems instead of hiding from them.

Confront backbiters and deriders. Have discussions with parents or in-laws in front of your spouse. As with your kids, make it uncomfortable to lie. When everyone is present, no one has to decide who to trust because everyone knows what was said and how it was stated. This ends the "he said, she said" style of manipulation common in many families. That sort of manipulation is designed to leave just enough doubt that you won't feel comfortable acting decisively because you could have heard the story wrong. When everyone hears it, there's consensus, and you can react with confidence that you're acting on the truth.

Most in-law problems come down to conflicting personal aesthetics, not important moral issues. This means the controlling in-laws have first manipulated themselves into believing that their aesthetics are morally superior to all others and that they should try to change a grown adult's preference to match their own. Once they can be persuaded that it's not worth their energy to aggressively attempt to "fix" someone over personal aesthetic differences, they can begin to love that person for the good that is in them.

Don't tolerate your parents' disrespect toward your spouse. You don't have to go in with guns blazing, but you do need to confront the problem and help fix that relationship. Don't leave your spouse to deal with your parents alone. That breaks the connection between spouses and allows your parents to dig in even deeper with their manipulation. Present a united front.

Resetting incentives is key. Talk with your manipulative family members and ask them what they really want. Then show them how to achieve those ends through persuasion instead of manipulation. Make that conversation completely transparent so they see how they're ruining their own hopes. Help them target new incentives and give them the appropriate way to reach that incentive. Guide them in taking the new direction under their own internal motivation.

How Can I Fight a Manipulator?

Don't. Resolve your problems without fighting.

If you enter the disagreement on the manipulator's terms, you've already lost. Manipulation relies on "me versus you" conflict because it's zero sum. Persuasion springs from abundance and allows everyone to win together.

The best way to combat manipulators is to be as open and honest as you can. Manipulation must remain hidden, or it'll stop working. Forcing manipulation to play out in the open is like dragging a vampire into the sunlight. Manipulation is unable to survive in the light of truth. Your openness is a weapon that strikes on its own.

How Do I Stop Manipulating My Own Children?

Before you can completely stop manipulating your children, you need to stop manipulating yourself. You need to dive deep into your mind, habits and beliefs, perhaps with the help of a coach or therapist. Look for areas where you are not living in a way aligned with truth. That's where you will find your self-manipulations.

Guilting and shaming aren't the only forms of manipulation. So is bribing. Authoritarian parenting and permissive parenting are two sides of the same coin. It's unfortunate that peaceful parenting communities online often recommend "sweet" manipulation. Buying compliance from loved ones is unhealthy. It follows a tactic similar to the niceness manipulation companies use on unsuspecting employees. "If you do this, then you'll get . . ." is a tell for manipulation in a household, as are reward checklists and other tactics that train children to prioritize rules over relationships and self-care. Creating opportunities and giving gifts to your child only to later use those as leverage to coerce them into behaving as you wish teaches them that nothing good is done out of love and that every gift has a cost. This undermines their ability to bond with and love others.

The solution? Help your children internalize and build their own motivation for the decisions they need to make. The first step is to throw away age-inappropriate expectations. Recognize that persuasion is about changing minds, not taking away privileges—including privileges you've invented. Persuasion is effective with kids as young as twelve months, maybe even younger for some.

Every mother who has soothed a crying infant knows that her gentle love, physical touch, and soft voice persuade her baby to settle down. This, too, is persuasion. It builds trust in the mother and sets the pattern for her to be effective at connecting with her child later in life.

Persuasion builds stronger bonds with children than rules do. It creates a feeling of security so strong that respecting you, pleasing you, and—when age appropriate—caring for themselves comes naturally. The connection *is* the reward.

Children who feel insecure because of your prior behavior may initially resist persuasion. They're testing to see if you're legitimately different. Give it time. Your patience and persistence will show them you're sincere, and their heart will open to you once again.

Persuasion trains your child to think rather than to follow blindly. Enlist your kids in finding solutions to conflict. Help them get what they want, and you will get what you want.

If you make a promise, you must follow through. No exceptions. Keep your word, or your kids won't trust you.

FAQs about Business and Public Life Manipulation

Now let's switch gears from personal to professional.

Is It Ever OK to Tell a "Noble" Lie?

No! Even a white lie is well-intentioned manipulation that will lead to unintended consequences you cannot know ahead of time. It never goes well.

Athletes deny their use of performance-enhancing drugs because they don't want to be banned from their sport, lose their sponsorships, have their achievements invalidated, or encourage young fans to take steroids. But falsely crediting their success purely to hard work distorts young men's expectations for their bodies and sports performance. They crave the success of their idols and become determined to emulate them. When they get older and find out about athletes' steroid use anyway, the lies lead to an outcome worse than just telling the truth. An entire generation of athletes learn that success at the highest level is only possible through cheating. That's not true, but it's the story that "noble" lie told.

How Do I Make Employees Work Harder without Manipulating Them?

Fill your workplace with opportunity, win-win scenarios, and honesty. Remember how LEGO treats their employees like rock stars? I have never heard a LEGO employee say a bad word about the company. Some McDonald's franchise owners I've spoken with run their store this way, too. They offer their employees assistance with college and then incentivize them to stay on by guaranteeing a job for five years.

One of the most demotivating parts of most postindustrial jobs is never seeing the results of your hard work being enjoyed by the end consumer. There can be no "win" when there is no gain. People who believe that their work is making the world a better place don't need to be externally motivated. Help your people see the real, human good that they are doing when they act in a professional manner. Of course, this requires your company to be ethical.

Where people see no future with you and no greater good in their job, there cannot be a bond, and persuasion doesn't work. You've got to offer more than a paycheck.

How Do I Achieve My Maximum Potential?

The most common obstacle to a high-performance career is not uncertainty about what to do; it's doubt about your own ability to execute and deliver those results. Over time, this becomes a major impediment to performing at your best. It's like driving in the fast lane with one foot heavy on the brake. Chronic self-doubt has its own name—imposter syndrome.

Imposter syndrome is the pervasive feeling that everyone else around you is competent, but you reached your current position by sheer luck and don't belong. Even successful people experience imposter syndrome. In fact, I'd say it's more common that highly capable professionals feel like they are frauds.

So what's to be done? How do you take your foot off the brake and reach maximum speed? Consider why people experience self-doubt; they first had to manipulate themselves into thinking that way. You reached the level you have for a reason. *You* are that reason. Actual frauds get found out soon and often don't last a month on the job; it's obvious to everyone they can't handle it.

If you have reached any modicum of professional success, it's OK to take appropriate credit for it. It's more than OK. It's essential. You owe it to yourself to cherish that success. You need to understand what makes you succeed, then apply that over and over. As a result, you will get out of your own way, build the confidence needed, and perform at the level you know deep down you always could. Because you persuaded yourself into it—and out of self-manipulation.

How Can I Build and Protect Customer Loyalty?

Betraying customers breaks the relationship of trust. If you make a promise, honor it. Don't pretend you care about people or things you don't really care about. Any pretending you do will come back to haunt you when aspects of your pretend value system come into conflict with each other.

Keep your quality level and customer service high enough so that your customers want to keep buying from you. Sometimes this means openly admitting mistakes and fixing them.

It's hard to manipulate people who have healthy relationships with each other. Building proper business relationships will help your customers resist manipulation from competitors. Guard those relationships by being open and honest.

How Do I Protect My Reputation?

A relationship is a fortress. You need healthy, well-bonded relationships with anyone you would ever want to come to your defense. Otherwise, when they succumb to manipulation, so will you.

Accused public figures whose family, friends, and fans do not overwhelmingly rush to their defense lack what Adam Lane Smith calls "healthy attachment." The rest of us wonder why they lack that bond. What secrets keep them apart? Maybe the accusations are true.

You are only as safe as the community you're in. This is why the mafia's organization model works. If you mess with the boss's daughter, the whole organization puts you in the ground. This mentality is digitized now. You are safe if you are connected to good, dangerous people who can defend you in times of need.

Many times, a cancel mob target's powerful friends will lead a counter-mob against the accuser. Exposing the attacker's immoral, unethical, or illegal acts is considered fair game. This behavior is similar to the frontier justice of bygone years.

We have a choice: either return to Wild West–style retribution or defend against manipulation. This book promotes the peaceful option whenever possible.

Since World War I, governments have abandoned persuasion for manipulation. They must hold on to their power with lies or violence. The public is only following their leaders in becoming more manipulative and aggressive. It will get worse before it gets better. But it will eventually get better if we the people demand it.

What's the Best Way to Navigate Woke Culture?

I spoke with the founders of a large multigenerational European company who expect a violent backlash against woke culture and organizations that have supported it. There is still some hope for a peaceful outcome. In the meantime, remain a clean, wholesome company that takes care of your employees and stay away from taking social stances. The upper class in business expect the backlash, and the wiser ones use persuasion within their companies and among employees so unhelpful activism will never stain their reputations.

Why did woke culture overtake so many multibillion-dollar companies? It's a sleight of hand to divert attention from their unethical and illegal business practices. They use identity politics to manipulate your attention away from these shady dealings.

Woke culture thrives on GSRRM—guilting people for their skin color, shaming them for attraction to people of the opposite sex, and undermining the country itself. One Microsoft diversity director reminded hundreds of people at a conference that the United States is racist, sexist, and still a beneficiary of slavery. Yet he never bothered to explain how he, a man of African descent, could have risen to the executive ranks of a Fortune 500 company if those things were still prevalent.

The Soviet Union fell because its manipulation stopped working. Things got bad enough that most people were forced to see through the lies. Don't fall into woke culture's manipulation trap, or you'll become a manipulator yourself.

Where will you be when the woke wall comes crashing down? Where will your company be? If your career or company culture is based on mutual manipulation and ideas that suddenly become unfashionable, you will pay a high price.

How Can Whistleblowers Survive?

In October 2021, an Australian state premier got caught taking tens of millions from Pfizer.[16] She resigned but defiantly stated that people should place certainty in leadership during COVID above other concerns. She responded like a typical political sociopath.

Manipulators are shameless. They only respond to force, and they will shift the blame whenever possible. They'll even blame the people who catch them, like Lance Armstrong did when he was caught using performance-enhancing drugs.

Whistleblowers often take flak. The offender's other victims may even join in on the attack because they're too manipulated to admit they have been fooled. Social status is the next most important need after physical survival. Attacking someone they are loyal to or work for is akin to attacking them.

VC Tim Draper said, "We have taken down another great icon," referring to embattled Theranos CEO

---

[16] Kirsty Needham, "Australia's NSW State Premier Resigns over Corruption Probe amid COVID-19 Battle," Reuters, October 1, 2021, https://www.reuters.com/world/asia-pacific/australian-state-corruption-watchdog-says-is-investigating-nsw-premier-2021-10-01/.

Elizabeth Holmes.[17] She was charged by the SEC for fraud spanning years in an elaborate scheme to lie to the entire world. But no, her fraud wasn't the problem. We took away a role model for young women. In Tim Draper's eyes, we should have let the manipulation continue indefinitely.

Bank employees who steal six figures or more are paid to quit or even given "promotions" to non-sensitive positions because banks cannot let the theft of depositors' money become public. It makes you wonder how many bank CEOs gained their positions by stealing eight figures.

If it was pointed out you have been manipulating your family, you'd probably resist coming clean. Most likely, you'd fear losing your wife and children. Manipulation is a trap. It only gets worse until manipulators take the pain and extract themselves.

Whether in a company or organization, if you notice manipulation but say nothing about it, you, too, will be consumed by it. Either you expose it or you become a target.

At first, people respond poorly. The first accuser is the attacker. The first whistleblower is a threat. Nobody believed Monica Lewinsky until more women came out with credible stories.

---

[17] Polina Marinova, "Why VC Tim Draper Keeps Defending Theranos CEO Elizabeth Holmes," *Fortune*, May 11, 2018, https://fortune.com/2018/05/11/tim-draper-theranos-elizabeth-holmes/.

My guidance to whistleblowers is this: prepare for the consequences either way. Both choices have costs, including loss of reputation, marriage, children, livelihood, and even life. Which are you willing to pay? The pain of not acting must be greater than the pain of acting.

Alternative medicine doctors have been murdered in the past few years in the West.[18] Now, some people wonder if those killings are linked to the COVID shutdown. Because we have a manipulative government, we have to wonder. How far will the manipulators go to protect their lies? Whistleblowers need to ask themselves this question and prepare for the worst.

Consider the king's court. A jester could tell the truth without losing his head. At worst, he could spend time in a dungeon if his jokes went too far. Now, comedians who speak candidly and sincerely get the book thrown at them. This explains the high demand for dissident memes on social media. *The Babylon Bee* is as popular as *The Onion* once was. They are telling the truth with laughter.

Truth with mirth is one approach to whistleblowing. The other is appealing to people's virtue. You have to choose whether you'll be the hero or the villain's henchman. Remember how often henchmen become victims.

Many whistleblower stories follow the mythic template of the hero's journey. Most initially reject the call

---

[18] "Six Doctors Found Dead under Suspicious Circumstances," CBS12 News, August 28, 2015, https://cbs12.com/news/local/six-doctors-found-dead-under-suspicious-circumstances.

to be a hero. They try to rationalize the decision. The difference is that afterward, real heroes change their minds and answer the call. Then they look for allies, build strength, find out who they really are, and press through to victory.

Sometimes, the most heroic act is to tell the truth because that just might threaten your personal safety. Consider the Book of Esther. Haman tried to get Esther and her family killed, but Esther connected with King Xerxes, and he fell in love with her. Then she revealed Haman's plot to murder her. Haman was punished for threatening a woman Xerxes loved. The manipulator did not count on someone telling the truth. When he realized what was happening, he panicked. Then it was over for Haman.

Esther told the truth and had an ally she did not expect—the gentile king, her husband. She was ready to resist manipulation before she laid it all on the line. So how can you prepare yourself? Reread and study the Defense against Manipulation chapter, knowing that you will be attacked by manipulators. Whether you appeal to virtue, crack a joke, tell the bold truth, or all three, you need to speak coherently. Include facts without spin and evidence instead of unsubstantiated claims. Let the story you're telling stir emotions without name-calling. Do not resort to GSRRM to make your points.

If you are going to blow the whistle, write down your statement with clarity and brevity. Be clear about your desired outcome. For example, if you find someone embezzling funds, you want his embezzlement stopped, law enforcement involved, and the same crime prevented from happening again.

The 1974 Portuguese Revolution, the French Revolution, and the Arab Spring show what happens when people organize against manipulators without clear goals. The end of manipulation created a power vacuum, which was filled by worse manipulators. Only the threat of American involvement kept communists from seizing power in Portugal.

After you write your report, distribute it to as many people as possible. The truth must be well publicized and so incensing that people cannot help but act. Publishing your story protects you by making the issue no longer your problem. It's the shareholders' problem, the media's problem, the law's problem. Manipulators cannot come after you if they are too busy defending themselves.

If you can deliver the report anonymously and still be taken seriously, do it. Give it to people who have a stake in the truth coming out. Otherwise, you'll make yourself a target.

Remember that lies are difficult and expensive to maintain. Shining the light of truth multiplies that expense.

You have to fulfill your moral responsibilities or live with knowing that your silence enabled the manipulations to continue.

The idea of a single red pill is a false dichotomy. Neo had several smaller wake-up calls before he left the Matrix. Each one brought him closer to reality.

We can suffer as heroes or be bystanders and let our children suffer. Everyone's going to die eventually. Why not die with honor? Only you can make that choice. But remember: If not you, then who? If not now, then when?

How Should We All Respond to Mass Manipulation?

Politicians, unelected government officials, and the mass media use manipulation on us constantly. Even law enforcement has come under scrutiny by people of all political persuasions. Each year, an average of 410 police officers in the US are arrested for crimes committed while on duty.[19] That may seem insignificant relative to the 696,000 full-time law enforcement officers employed in the US. It is statistically insignificant but personally destructive. For example, in 2013, the West Valley City, Utah, police's narcotics team was disbanded as a result of crime. Officers stole private property from seized vehicles, hid evidence, and placed

[19] Philip Matthew Stinson, Sr., John Liederbach, Steven P. Lab, and Steven L. Brewer, Jr., *Police Integrity Lost: A Study of Law Enforcement Officers Arrested* (Washington, DC: US Department of Justice, 2016), https://www.ojp.gov/pdffiles1/nij/grants/249850.pdf.

tracking devices on potential suspects' vehicles without warrants. We wouldn't know about this if they hadn't gotten caught. And how many don't? It's not "insignificant" if a single person's civil rights are ignored by a single police officer.

Protection from manipulative law enforcement is essential to the American ethos. The United States' founding fathers gave citizens the Fifth Amendment to protect them from manipulative law enforcement. This amendment to the US Constitution reads:

No person shall be held to answer for a capital, or otherwise infamous crime, unless on a presentment or indictment of a Grand Jury, except in cases arising in the land or naval forces, or in the Militia, when in actual service in time of War or public danger; nor shall any person be subject for the same offence to be twice put in jeopardy of life or limb; nor shall be compelled in any criminal case to be a witness against himself, nor be deprived of life, liberty, or property, without due process of law; nor shall private property be taken for public use, without just compensation.[20]

Unethical law enforcement during British colonial rule was a problem the founders did not want repeated in the young constitutional republic. Professional, impartial

---

[20] United States Constitution, The Constitute Project, 1789 (rev. 1992), https://www.constituteproject.org/constitution/United_States_of_America_1992.

law enforcement has remained an American value over the centuries, even though citizens have sometimes had to enforce that value. "Any lawyer worth his salt will tell [a] suspect in no uncertain terms to make no statement to police under any circumstances," said former US Supreme Court Justice Robert Jackson.[21] In other words, exercise the right to remain silent, or you may be manipulated into confessing to a crime you did not commit.

Refusing to incriminate yourself may work in the rare situation when you are questioned by police. What about those other examples of mass manipulation? The president? Major media? Big tech? What if your voice is too small? What if someone you love is caught in manipulation? Confronting someone about it puts your relationship in danger—people are getting divorced over disagreements about mask mandates and vaccine requirements.

Your best course of action is taking the steps I mention in this book. Make yourself strong against manipulation. Teach others through example and through clear instructions. Have them read this book. Spread the word about persuasion versus manipulation. Eventually, persuasion will win.

---

[21] Mark Moller, "The End of 'The Right to Remain Silent,'" The Cato Institute, June 8, 2004, https://www.cato.org/commentary/end-right-remain-silent.

And don't let the mass manipulators manipulate you through your loved ones. Apply the same boundaries to them as you would with others. Keep yourself strong so they see an alternative to the lies they've been fed. Setting a good example is your best hope of helping them wake up to the truth.

EPILOGUE: CREATING A HIGH-TRUST WORLD

When you started reading this book, you knew something wasn't right. Someone in your life or in your past had done things that didn't make sense. Why would someone want to hurt other people? Why manipulate? Why not just be honest?

Through the course of this book, you've learned the answers. Most people manipulate when they're afraid. When they don't know a better way. And some people do learn better but refuse to stop. The power becomes addictive. There is true evil in this world, and knowing that isn't enough. We must build protections into our relationships to defend us from bad actors.

You learned to build those protections. In your workplace, in your friendships, and even in your family, you identified new methods and enacted plans to keep yourself and your loved ones safe from manipulation.

And you learned how to push back against manipulation attempts ethically. Because it's not enough to play defense. You want to make a better world. Now you've got the tools to do so.

This book didn't just prepare you to deal with a bad boss or an angry parent. You are armed to wage war against the manipulations you'll see in the world. All those times you saw ugliness and said, "I wish I could do something about this"—now you can. You are no longer helpless. And you don't have to hunker down and endure. You can act. You can go on the offense.

And I hope you do. A better world built on respect and persuasion could be one generation away. And we can create that generation in the next few years—with our families, friends, and coworkers.

The stand you take matters. When you say no to manipulation, you toss a stone into the pond. That stone causes ripples that spread from the site of impact. That's how truth and persuasion spread from you. The moment you make yourself immune to manipulation and stop manipulating others, you create a highly competitive center of trust. I say *competitive* because you create a desirable network that others will see and value. You offer competition to the manipulative networks by entering the social market with a tremendously desirable offer that few will turn down. Most people will see the difference and abandon the evil for the good.

A high-trust environment built on persuasion has far more power than we think. Like-minded people see it and are desperate to join. They grow the bubble of persuasion and trust.

These bubbles form a village, then a state, then a nation. If a million people participate, a million impact sites spread a million sets of ripples. Eventually, these high-trust environments meet and unite, and we've changed the world for the better.

High-trust societies have been built before. Every traditional European society and many East Asian cultures achieved this. It's how they developed into functioning community in the first place. But many of those societies utilized retributive interpersonal violence to suppress manipulative behaviors and thereby instill trust. If people ripped you off, you found them, punched them, and drove them out of town forever. We don't want to recreate that because it leads to costly cycles of revenge.

But we need something in its place. Our society rejected interpersonal violence and domesticated physical aggression, leading to a more peaceful community. Then the lack of physical consequences made room for a more subtle form of violence, a violation of the mind—manipulation. Now manipulation is threatening that peace. We are back to looking for solutions, and some are calling for a return to retributive violence.

We want to break the cycle without allowing either unshackled violence or manipulation to undermine our society. This is why we need to replace manipulation with persuasion: so we don't revert back to retaliation through physical violence or psychological manipulation. Persuasion ends the threat of both.

We can build a healthy world based on persuasion instead of manipulation. It begins with you, and it starts today.

Thank you for letting me teach you about persuasion. To continue your journey toward a manipulation-free world, check out more resources at www.unbreakable-mindconsulting.com.

You've learned persuasion. Now learn how to be a persuasive spouse, parent, employee, and leader. My personal persuasion course teaches you targeted methods to change your manipulative behaviors. If you want to work with me one-on-one, I also offer coaching with a free introductory session.

No need to leave positivity at home. Ensure your organization stands the test of time. My organizational coaching practice can help you free your office, club, or team from manipulation.

Your journey begins here. Replace your conditioning to manipulate yourself and others with persuasive behaviors. The change will make all the difference in your quality of life. And that will help you replace manipulation with persuasion and build a high-trust world.

Don't be intimidated. You were made to persuade. The power is in your hands. It always was.

Never let anyone manipulate you again.

WHAT'S NEXT?

This book reveals the manipulation around you. This new course teaches you what to do about it.

Unbreakable Mind is a video course that trains you to respond to manipulation with persuasion and does so with word-for-word scripts and numerous real-world examples.

In short, what this book tells you, the course shows.

Give yourself an unbreakable mind.

Resist manipulation.

Persuade with integrity.

And make people deal with you honestly.

Readers get 40 percent off—Use discount code IMMUNE.

ACKNOWLEDGMENTS

Thank you to my wife, Raquel, who, in retrospect, I married because she was not a manipulative woman.

Thank you to my son, Levi, who has boldly called out manipulation whenever he sees it since he could speak. This included helping me stop some points of self-manipulation.

Thank you also to Francis for his support and feedback, which helped me see where my explanations assumed too much knowledge on the reader's part.

And thank you to my great-grandmother, who impressed upon me that our family religion was the worship of truth, which is the antidote to manipulation.

ABOUT THE AUTHOR

Noah Revoy is a personal and business relationship strategist who teaches individuals and organizations how to identify and resist manipulation. Noah mentors couples, professionals, founders, executives, and investors to build sustainable, win-win relationships.

Everyone who deals with thousands of people over decades notices patterns. Over and over, Noah saw that people he cared about suffered from the same manipulative attacks. Simply noticing the recurrence empowered him to accurately identify and protect himself and others. Noah compiled what he learned into *Become Immune to Manipulation*, his second book. Find additional resources to counter manipulation with ethical persuasion at www.unbreakablemindconsulting.com.